Navigating the challenges of digital transformation in the world of AI

Diljeet Saluja

Printed in India

IndiePress

ISBN: 978-93-6045-227-8

First Printing, 2025

IndiePress

A division of Nasadiya Technologies Private Ltd.

Koramangala, Bangalore

Karnataka-560029

http://indiepress.in/

Edited by Literary Connect

Typesetting by MAP Systems, Bangalore

Publishing Consultant: Rechal Fernandes

Book Cover Design by Hude studio

Contents

Foreword - 1 vii

Foreword - 2 ix

Praise for "Navigating Challenges of Digital Transformation in the world of AI" xi

Special Gratitude xxv

Acknowledgments xxix

Preface xxxiii

My Journey xxxiii

Who should read this book? xxxvii

How is the book flow designed? xxxix

Chapter 1: The fast-evolving world of Digital Transformation 1

Chapter 2: Industry Leaders' Perspectives - Insights from Leadership Survey 11

Chapter 3: Understanding Client and Tech Partner Maturity Spectrum 25

Chapter 4: Why do clients think the way they do? 35

Chapter 5: Exploring Commercial Models in Digital Transformation 53

Chapter 6: Executing Digital Transformation within Constraints 83

Chapter 7: The Art and Science of Change Management 129

Chapter 8: Leadership Styles for Large-Scale Transformation 145

Chapter 9: Revenue Recognition in Transformation Programs 157

Chapter 10: Glossary and Index 171

Foreword - 1

Digital transformation has never been a walk in the park for even the most sophisticated firms; while the end goal may seem to be familiar, the journey for each has been fraught with unique sets of challenges. And those in charge of leading such transformation have been veritable explorers for much of the journey, beset with multiple challenges of the unknown. The transformation journey undertaken by firms over the past couple of decades has been driven by multiple waves of technological advances like digital, smartphones, digital marketing, big data, microservices, cloud computing. The latest wave of Artificial Intelligence (AI) is probably most promising and also the most disruptive yet. AI has the potential to significantly reimagine ways of working and to enhance productivity, yet its complexity and intangibility add a shroud of mystery to already complicated transformation programs. Diljeet Saluja's *Navigating the Challenges of Digital Transformation in the world of AI* presents a seminal compendium of strategies and tactics to navigate the complexities of large digital transformation programs especially as AI emerges as the key pivot for innovation in the modern times.

Saluja has been a key practitioner in the space of digital technology for nearly three decades, and his experience extends across multiple high-profile and complex transformation programs that he has led or been parachuted in to rescue and turn around. Always a keen observer of patterns, the author has been in the forefront of demystifying and thereby reducing risk profiles of such programs for his clients. In this work, the author builds a soup-to-nuts narrative and uses the metaphor of cooking a delectable dish using the right ingredients at the right times, and presents a recipe for successful digital transformations. Saluja enriches this book with myriads of real-life examples drawn from his - and others' - vast experience in leading large programs that met their business goals and built successful careers for sponsors and those involved alike.

I wholeheartedly recommend this book to a broad audience from someone new to the field who has a large transformation program thrust upon them to seasoned executives. Its pages promise not only knowledge and practical guidance, but also offer a wealth of perspectives that can only come from the experiences built over many long nights of brainstorms and reviews. This book is essential reading for anyone keen to learn the intricacies that differentiate large programs, manage risks of running digital initiatives, and leading meaningful engagements with an eye to disrupting the status quo.

Shubhradeep Guha

Chief Delivery Officer, Publicis Sapient

Foreword - 2

Diljeet's journey began as a young civil engineer on a remote island in the Maldives, where he learned the true meaning of project management under challenging conditions. His career evolved from construction to technology, driven by a passion for growth and innovation. Over three decade, Diljeet has managed over 45 engagements across multiple continents, delivering large-scale tech solutions and mentoring countless colleagues. His experiences and insights, rooted in honesty, integrity, and the power of relationships, form the foundation of this book, "Navigating the Challenges of Digital Transformation in the World of AI."

My perspective to this book may be very unique because I not only had had the opportunity to closely partner with Diljeet on a larger transformative digital transformation project for a large Indian Conglomerate's Global Education Business, but have had the opportunity to deliver such transformative – digital first in my past assignments. Hence, some of these learning that Diljeet share are "money can't buy" wisdom and priceless !

In the new normal, dynamic landscape of technology, digital transformation epitomizes progress and innovation. Over the past three decades, we've transitioned from monolithic mainframes to agile, AI-driven methodologies. This book, serves as a comprehensive guide through this journey, offering invaluable insights and practical wisdom. Diljeet's book masterfully demystifies the complexities of digital transformation by breaking it down into nine well-structured chapters, each offering actionable insights and strategies.

It begins by tracing technological advancements over the past 30 years, providing historical context and laying the groundwork for understanding the evolution of digital transformation. The narrative then delves into the priorities and challenges faced by industry leaders, presenting valuable insights from a comprehensive leadership survey.

The book explores the varying maturity levels of clients and technology partners, highlighting how these differences influence the success of transformation efforts. It provides a deep dive into the thought processes and mental models of key decision-makers, offering clarity on how these perspectives shape projects. Practical advice follows, with a detailed discussion of commercial models, helping readers navigate the complexities of selecting the right approach for their unique needs.

The focus then shifts to execution, offering strategies for overcoming constraints related to budget, time, and scope. Change management is given thoughtful attention, emphasizing why people resist change and how to navigate it effectively. Leadership traits essential for driving large-scale transformations are explored, and the bonus chapter provides critical insights into revenue recognition.

As you embark on this journey through the pages of this book, I hope you find the insights and strategies presented both enlightening and actionable. Digital transformation is not merely a technological shift; it is a profound cultural and organizational evolution. By embracing its complexities and applying the lessons shared, we can pave the way for a future that is innovative, resilient, and sustainable.

Jose Leon

Chief Executive Office - Densu X

Praise for "Navigating Challenges of Digital Transformation in the world of AI"

This book is a rich read. I was once on a discovery trip with Diljeet to the TajMahl, located on the right bank of the Yamuna River in Agra, Uttar Pradesh, India I distinctly remember our discussion about architecture and the nuances of building the Taj Mahal. His book takes a similar creative approach to the transformation journey in which he provides simple yet effective instructions, including how to scale the critical nuanced hurdles in the world of digital, data and AI.

It recognizes that transformation is not just a technical architectural model that can help you drive greater value. It is a practical guide that integrates art and science to encourage and drive value across the business and opens the door to an improved operating model capable of putting transformation ownership in the right hands and creating a digital ecosystem of continuous value exchange as the end product. "In essence putting the science where the art happens." Thanks for crafting and sharing your knowledge and experience.

Greg Austin
Senior Vice President, Thoughtworks
Dallas USA

★★★

I had the pleasure of working alongside Diljeet, and I'm thrilled to recommend his latest book, *"Navigating the Challenges of Digital Transformation in the World of AI"*. Drawing on 3+ decades of software delivery leadership experience, he has crafted a novel mental model that evolves over time, making it a valuable guide for real-world practitioners.

The book is packed with real-world examples, templates, and methods that effectively navigate the complexities of multi-modal digital transformation. While digital transformation is often seen as a domain reserved for management veterans running multi-million-dollar, large-scale projects with 100s or 1000s of people, this book offers a unique and insightful "secret recipe" for technologists. It equips them with the tools and knowledge to tackle real-world challenges, helping them build confidence to tackle large scale transformation and make there way into top management.

For the true tech enthusiasts out there, you might view AI as just a buzzword in the title, but rest assured, the principles discussed in this book are timeless. These concepts will remain relevant long after the current waves of AI evolution have passed.

Highly recommend this book to anyone interested in mastering digital transformation from a practical, technologist's perspective!

Abhinav Gupta
Global Head of Engineering and
Country Head, Bravura India
Gurgaon India

★★★

Diljeet's book is a true study of the theoretical and more importantly practical concepts that underpin the dynamics of managing a large-scale digital transformation, while managing disruptions and industry headwinds. His perspective on AI's growing presence and its role in our development methodologies is both a cautionary tale of pitfalls for the unprepared while shining a light on the limitless possibilities when deployed appropriately and effectively. His ability to also wear the hat of the informed and courageous executive provides valuable insights that are precise, action-provoking and grounded in decades of experience.

He also generously weaves in best practices and techniques to address a wide array of challenges, of the highest degrees of complexity in the most tenuous environments. Whether that is applying a rigorous lens to the client's digital fluency and maturity to leveraging the appropriate commercial models to create win-win engagements. The pinnacle of excellence and execution is usually embedded in the degree of discipline we bring into our governance. If you were not excited about change management before, it's time to get excited. This book offers a perspective on the human side of change while offering a structured, yet compassionate approach to communicating, managing and enabling measurable and enduring change.

This book is a comprehensive guide for any technologist, practice lead, executive or individual contributor to inform their strategies and ultimately, apply a common sense approach to executing on their ideas. Lastly, this compilation of principles and vetted techniques, it is a true stand-out. It is able to translate hard-earned lessons into simple, relatable guidance. It's not a theory-heavy tome; it's hands-on, from the field, and full of the kinds of insight that only come from years in the trenches of digital transformation.

Vi Nguyen
Engineering Partner, Thoughtworks
Dallas USA

★★★

"Navigating the Challenges of Digital Transformation in the world of AI" is a valuable and thought-provoking read for business executives, technologists, and change agents looking to better understand the complexities of digital transformation in this Era. The book is a commendable attempt at demystifying Digital beyond the jargon, highlighting its practical application, strategic significance, and the necessary culture shift.

The narrative begins by positioning Digital at the center of the Fourth Industrial Revolution, emphasizing that digital transformation is not simply a technological advance but a redefinition of the manner organizations operate, make decisions, and interact with customers. From understanding the client mental models to chnage managemet and hyper-personalized interactions, the book chronicles some of the most significant steps needed to be on top of the game.

This is a special book because it is balanced on the one hand with optimism and on the other with realism. This is a readable and useful handbook for anyone navigating the intricate terrain of digital change during the era of AI. It is a worthwhile addition for any library of leaders, with strategic ideas combined with practical advice.

Lalit Mehta
CEO, Co-Founder, Decimal Technologies
Gurgaon India

★★★

Diljeet is a brilliant technocrat, a natural leader, an inspiring teacher, and a captivating storyteller. His book is a comprehensive and insightful guide to navigating digital transformation in the complex world of AI. With a holistic approach, he deconstructs Digital into smaller, digestible modules, making it easier to understand and implement. The book outlines actionable strategies that empower stakeholders to seamlessly integrate AI into their businesses for digital transformation. Without a doubt, AI will be a force multiplier for businesses, organizations, and society in the years to come.

While many books focus solely on technology, Diljeet goes beyond, projecting light on every facet of digital transformation. He masterfully explains the evolution of IT, the challenges of digital transformation, industry insights, customer experiences, and the maturity spectrum of clients and partners.

His analogy of a house representing various Digital building blocks is particularly fascinating. This structured, modular approach simplifies complex concepts, making it easily understandable to both beginners and experienced professionals alike. Whether you're a business leader or a technical architect, this book provides invaluable guidance for adopting AI-driven digital initiatives. As Digital transformation accelerates, it will increasingly separate industry leaders from those struggling to keep up.

Having had the privilege of working alongside Diljeet, I can vouch for his ability to challenge the status quo, bring fresh perspectives, and always see the bigger picture. He is a visionary who deeply understands how technology can be a powerful enabler and problem solver.

This book is a must-read for anyone looking to harness the power of digital transformation in an unchartered territory of AI world.

N K Jain
Partner Positive Momentum, Ex-CIO SBG
Gurgaon India

★★★

This book by Diljeet is extremely valuable for anyone involved in or embarking on digital transformation initiatives. The strategies and tactics in the book are relevant and relatable, as we navigate the complexities of large digital transformation programs with AI emerging as a crucial driver of change and innovation. Diljeet has drawn on his extensive experience to provide invaluable insights and does this in a way which keeps the reader engaged. The examples make complex concepts comprehensible and enable one to act on and apply the learnings. I found the chapters on commercial models and revenue recognition invaluable and very pertinent.

Saptorsi Hore
SVP, Global Head of Operation Excellence, Thoughtworks
Bangalore India

★★★

Who knew a non-techie like me would be hooked on a book about digital transformation? On the face of it, this is a deep dive into the tech industry — but at its core, it's about navigating uncertainty, making decisions in a foggy future, and managing change with finesse.

As an academician and master coach, I discovered plenty of insights that resonate well beyond the realm of technology. Diljeet's storytelling and sharp observations break industry boundaries, offering lessons that apply to leadership, strategy, and change management across sectors.

Dr. Arvinder Kaur Pabla
Deputy Director, CEAPS, SGT University &
Master Coach in Behavioural and Soft Skill
Gurgaon India

★★★

The book expertly guides readers through modern organizational decision-making challenges by presenting strategic insights alongside practical frameworks. It offers a detailed examination of the 'Done is better than perfect' and 'First Time Right' methods while presenting an objective view of how these approaches affect speed control quality, and risk management. Saluja demonstrates through detailed case studies and authentic examples how executives such as CIOs, CDOs, and business leaders can manage priorities to foster innovation while maintaining a balance between speed and quality. This book is essential reading for professionals who need to achieve both agility and precision in today's fast-paced business world.

Amar Karande
Partner, Head of Private Equity Syntax
California USA

★★★

In an era where digital transformation is both a necessity and a challenge, this book serves as an essential guide for professionals navigating the complexities of AI-driven change. With 3 decades of hands-on experience distilled into practical wisdom, the author provides invaluable insights into transformation drivers, client decision-making, deal structuring, execution methodologies, and change management. Whether you're a program manager, delivery partner, architect, or developer, this book equips you with the knowledge and frameworks needed to drive successful transformations. A must-read for anyone looking to turn strategy into execution with confidence and clarity.

Amit Chhabra
EVP, Head of Digital and CX, SBI Cards
Delhi India

★★★

This book is like having a trusted mentor walk you through the highs and lows of leading digital transformation, especially in today's AI-driven world. It starts by giving you a sense of how far we've come in technology (Chapter 1) and then dives into the real challenges leaders face, like juggling priorities and dealing with differing maturity levels among teams (Chapters 2 and 3). If you've ever struggled with decision-making or felt stuck trying to align stakeholders, Chapter 4 offers clarity on leadership mindsets that can make or break a project. The book also gets super practical, with advice on picking the right commercial models (Chapter 5) and overcoming execution hurdles like budget and time constraints (Chapter 6). Change management (Chapter 7) and leadership traits (Chapter 8) are explored in a way that feels relatable, with actionable tips you can apply immediately. And if you're a numbers person, the bonus chapter on revenue recognition ties it all together. Whether you're new to this space or a seasoned pro, this book feels like a conversation with someone who's been in the trenches—and has the scars to prove it.

Charith Tangirala
Market Tech Director, Thoughtworks
Dallas USA

★★★

Diljeet's maiden book *'Navigating the Challenges of Digital Transformation'* approaches Digital transformation in a holistic way, seeing the transformation through the lens of commercials, technology, clients, change management etc. The book speaks the language of a 'practioner' who has done multiple digital transformations and yet the concepts are demystified using less jargons. The chapter on clients is my favourite as most of the books on transformation treat clients as 'yet another entity', while they should occupy the center stage. I highly recommend this book to get a multi dimensional understanding of Digital transformation for being grounded and yet insightful.

Ramki Sitaraman
Engineering Partner, Thoughtworks
Chennai, India

★★★

This book starts on familiar ground—the evolution of software development—but quickly expands into the broader, often complex world of digital transformation. It connects the dots between well-known mechanics and the less familiar aspects of execution at scale. Having spent only part of my career in consulting, I found the structured breakdowns, AI impact framing, and distinctions between leadership roles (CTO/CIO/CDO) particularly insightful.

The discussion on key ingredients for large transformation programs, trade-offs, and the practical tools and techniques was especially valuable. I appreciated how it emphasized articulating value continuously, though I would have loved to see more on operationalizing trade-off decisions. The change management framework, D x V x F x S > R, was new to me, but it really resonated.

This book provides a much-needed top-down view for those navigating digital transformation, helping them step back from the trees to see the entire forest. A compelling and highly practical read.

Jason Roberts
Technology Principal, Thoughtworks
New York, USA

★★★

Diljeet's book is a timely and essential guide to digital transformation in the AI era. As industries strive to keep pace with rapid advancements, this book bridges the gap between Digital-driven transformation and the challenges organizations face in adapting to change.

Drawing from over 30 years of experience in digital transformation, spanning agile development to AI-first software development, Diljeet offers deep industry insights into how organizations and their partners can mature and lead the future of digital transformation. The book delves into critical aspects such as commercial and revenue management, the complexities of large-scale transformations, and the importance of aligning efforts with business value.

In an era where the only constant is change, agility is crucial. This book explores the constraints and challenges of managing transformation while maintaining agility. More importantly, it highlights the key traits that stakeholders and organizations must develop to successfully navigate this evolving landscape.

Through real-world experiences and firsthand accounts from IT professionals, Diljeet provides invaluable lessons on the challenges and opportunities that lie ahead in an AI-driven world. This book not only prepares readers for what's coming but also illustrates how AI can be leveraged to drive meaningful and sustainable transformation.

Kuldeep Singh
Principal Consultant, Emerging Technologies, Thoughtworks
Author, "Exploring the Metaverse - Redefining Reality in the Digital Age"
Gurgaon, India

★★★

"Navigating the Challenges of Digital Transformation in the World of AI" by Diljeet Saluja is a masterful guide that bridges the gap between theoretical concepts and practical implementation in the complex realm of digital transformation. Drawing from nearly three decades of hands-on experience across multiple continents, Diljeet offers readers a comprehensive roadmap for navigating the intricacies of large-scale technological change.

This book stands out for its unique blend of historical context, strategic insights, and actionable advice. Diljeet's approach of using the metaphor of cooking a delectable dish to explain the nuances of digital transformation is both innovative and highly effective.

His real-life examples and case studies provide invaluable lessons that can only come from years of experience in the field.

The book's well-structured chapters cover everything from understanding varying maturity levels of clients and partners to navigating complex commercial models and overcoming execution constraints. For anyone involved in or interested in digital transformation, whether you're a seasoned executive or new to the field, this book is an essential read. It not only demystifies the complexities of large-scale digital programs but also provides a clear framework for success in an AI-driven world. Diljeet's work is designed to become a go-to resource for those seeking to lead meaningful and impactful digital transformations in the modern era.

Sameer Gaikwad
Vice President Customer Success, VirtualHealth
Philadelphia, USA

★★★

"Navigating the Challenges of Digital Transformation in the World of AI" is an essential guide for professionals looking to thrive in the rapidly evolving digital landscape. With a keen focus on practical insights and real-world applications, this book demystifies the complexities of AI-driven digital transformation, offering strategic frameworks, case studies, and actionable guidance. Whether you're a business leader, IT strategist, or digital transformation consultant, this book equips you with the knowledge while addressing challenges like change management, ethical considerations, and technology adoption. A must-read for anyone seeking to drive innovation and stay ahead in the AI era!

Kapil Suri
Vice President, Nextuple Inc
Gurgaon, India

★★★

Diljeet, What struck me the most in the Book was Q&A kind of format, instruction-focused approach and story telling style.

I also liked how you highlighted the tension between different members of the C suite. Different mental models is a big source of the friction in the C-suite. I think that's true to an extent. And it's a worthwhile to note that people can be more effective when they understand what the person across the table is trying to accomplish.

Evan Kramer
Director Solution Engineering,
The Modern Data Company
New Jearsey, USA

★★★

If you're a working professional wondering how to keep up with all the changes Digital is bringing, this book is a great place to start.

What I really liked is how simple and clear the writing is. Diljeet Saluja doesn't try to impress you with big words. He explains things in a way that makes sense, using real examples from different companies and situations.

This book is especially helpful if you're trying to understand how to make new tools and technology work in your team or company- without losing sight of the people who make it all possible. It's not just for tech folks; anyone in business, leadership, or even just figuring out their career path will find something useful here. Easy to read, practical, and very relevant to the world we're working in today.

Gaurav Sabharwal
Co-Founder & CEO, JOP
New Delhi, India

★★★

Diljeet does a fantastic job of explaining digital transformation in a clear and structured way. This book makes a complex topic easy to understand, providing valuable insights for business leaders, technology experts, and digital strategists. By sharing real-world experiences, industry trends, and practical advice, Diljeet helps readers navigate the challenges of AI-driven change. Whether you are making big decisions or working on implementation, this book will be a great guide.

Wishing Diljeet great success with this book and looking forward to many more insightful books in the future!

Sanjeev Krishnan
Founder, Vantlogix
Dubai, UAE

Special Gratitude

For Shubhradeep Guha

I am deeply grateful to Shubhradeep Guha, a mentor and guide who has profoundly influenced my personal and professional journey. Our time together during the final four years of my nine-year tenure at Sapient was transformative. As a Client Executive and Delivery Lead for APAC accounts, I had the privilege of collaborating with Shubhra on building Sapient's India footprint. Under his leadership, I learned invaluable lessons that reshaped my approach to problem-solving and leadership.

Shubhra's brilliance lies in his extraordinary ability to think beyond the obvious. Before meeting him, "thinking out of the box" was just a buzzword to me. Shubhra turned it into a way of life. His scenario analysis skills are unparalleled—he could dissect the most complex challenges and guide you toward innovative, actionable solutions that seemed both cutting-edge and inevitable.

Even after I left Sapient, Shubhra remained a constant mentor, offering both professional and personal guidance. When I moved to Chicago in 2024 and he was in San Francisco with Google, I had the unique advantage of being in a similar time zone. Over several months, Shubhra dedicated 16-20 evenings, each lasting 2-3 hours, to provide invaluable feedback on my book, *Navigating the Challenges of Digital Transformation in the World of AI*. His insights shaped the book's narrative, and he graciously wrote its foreword.

Shubhra, your wisdom, generosity, and belief in me have been instrumental. This book stands as a testament to your mentorship, and for that, I am forever grateful.

Special Gratitude

For Jose Leon

I owe a heartfelt thanks to Jose Leon for his unwavering support and belief in my book. As the CEO of Dentsu X, his energy, business acumen, and thought leadership are truly unparalleled. Despite his demanding schedule, he took the time to provide invaluable insights, encouraging me to complete this journey and believing in the core strength of the book.

His creative ideas, especially around the book's online marketing and launch strategy, were transformative, giving the book a broader vision and reach. Having known Jose since 2012, when we represented Sapient and Adobe respectively, I have always been inspired by his ability to navigate complex challenges with clarity and innovation. Our exchanges on digital transformation across geographies have not only shaped my perspectives but also silently influenced many aspects of this book.

Jose's remarkable leadership, coupled with his willingness to guide and mentor, has been a driving force behind this endeavor. I am fortunate to have his encouragement and expertise shaping the book's journey. He is not just an exceptional professional but also a trusted collaborator and a true visionary.

Acknowledgments

While this book delves into the challenges faced during digital transformation, it has itself been a journey of transformation. Writing it was as much about discovery and growth as the topics it explores.

I must begin by expressing my deepest gratitude to Dr. Marshall Goldsmith, a visionary leader and a transformative thinker whose work has inspired millions, including me. Attending his workshop in Mumbai in January 2020 profoundly influenced my perspective on leadership and transformation. A chance meeting in Chicago rekindled our connection, and I am honored by his willingness to review this book and provide an endorsement. His encouragement and insights have been a guiding light throughout this journey.

Next, I want to acknowledge two remarkable women, Nisha Misra and Gunjan Shukla, trusted business leaders in Thoughtworks. Nisha identified the Fixed Bid SME in me and virtually parachuted me into a struggling program in NA, believing I held a magic wand. She stamped me as a Fixed Bid champion, which soon led Gunjan to ask me to coach leaders on this "scarce knowledge" within Thoughtworks. Gunjan further nudged me to write blogs, which evolved into a celebrated internal series. This journey led to designing an interactive workshop in the form of ILT (Instructor-Led Training). A heartfelt thanks to Abhinav Gupta and Vandana Sharma, who dared to co-train with me on this complex topic. Kuldeep Singh, with his laser-sharp insight, saw a book in this initiative, and Rajani Kafaltia, author of *Women Chin Up and Fix Yourself,* saw a writer in me.

This book was enriched through lunch meetings, coffee conversations, and backbench brainstorming sessions with my Gurgaon office colleagues: Rahul Koul, Anshul Gautam, Rupesh Ranjan, Mihir Katyanan, and Ankur Arora, whom Rahul affectionately calls "Servant Leaders."

Validating my ideas with senior Thoughtworks leaders was invaluable. My gratitude goes to Sudhir Tiwari and Sameer Soman for validating this as a topic of critical importance and to Sapto and Santosh for their sharp insights. Thanks to Sashi, Sandeep, Dinkar, Sumeet, Sachin, Ramki, Raghu, and KK for their constructive feedback that helped shape the narrative.

Thanks to Manish Sateeja for granting me the opportunity to work in the US, which not only expanded my perspective but also gave me the focus to write. Special thanks to the North America leadership team - Craig Stanley, Greg Austin, Vi Nguyen and to Amy Ludvig for providing a platform to test my ideas.

To my wife Rekha Saluja, and daughters, Gauri and Nandini, I owe more than words can express. Rekha took on the full weight of home and children, alongside her dream startup, Nordic Wonderkids, while I spent 10 months in the US to write this book. Gauri and Nandini lifted my spirits and helped refine illustrations, making the book better in countless ways.

Shubhra deserves special mention for challenging me to broaden the book's scope. Originally focused on Fixed Bid programs, his challenge led me to address the broader challenges in digital transformation execution. It was the most pivotal twist in this journey.

A heartfelt thanks to Shristee Publications for easing the pain of iterative editing and proofreading. Special thanks to Sudhindra for reviewing the initial cover page designs. And a big thank you to Sunny for helping me craft impactful LinkedIn posts to share this journey with the world.

Finally, huge kudos to Nazim Iqbal, my startup friend and founder of Hude Studio, for crafting a winning cover design. His human touch truly brought the book to life, living up to his reputation as a design genius.

I am grateful for the insights from Louise D. Bringselius' work, *Resistance to Change: Four Interpretations* (2010), which provided valuable perspectives on organizational change and its complexities. I also appreciate the foundational work of Richard Beckhard, David Gleicher, and later refinements by Dannemiller and Jacobs (1992) in shaping the D x V x F x S > R framework, which continues to provide valuable guidance for overcoming resistance to change.

Lastly, a small note to budding authors: writing a book is an evolution. Surround yourself with believers in your vision, remain open to feedback, and trust the process. Like they say, it takes nine months to deliver a baby; my book took ten, and now it's ready to see the daylight.

Preface

My Journey

It was midnight on December 12, 1994, and we were just an hour away from completing the final pour of concrete on the top floor of the Maldives Ports Authority (MPA) building. An archipelago in the Indian Ocean, the Maldives, is known for its stunning coral islands and clear waters. The MPA is a key hub for the country's maritime activities, making this project crucial for its infrastructure. This moment was significant not only because it marked the completion of the superstructure of this ship-shaped building, but also because it symbolized the end of my year-long assignment on the island of Malé. As the last of the concrete was laid, my team and I were ready to celebrate a hard-earned achievement.

When I landed in Malé in December 1993, I was a 22-year-old civil engineer with just six months of internship experience. My professional journey had begun in the newly developed colonies of Rohini in West Delhi, but here I was on a remote island in the Indian Ocean, with no mentor, no mobile phone, no YouTube tutorials, and no Google searches to rely on - just a stack of textbooks and a lot of determination. It was on this isolated island that I learned the true meaning of project management, navigating challenges that tested my skills and resilience.

As the year progressed, I not only learned the technical aspects of my job but also immersed myself in the local culture, picking up colloquial Divehi, the language spoken in the Maldives. I created my first project plan using Critical Path Method (CPM) and Program Evaluation and Review Technique (PERT), made tough decisions like persuading the Director of Civil Construction to trim 64 concrete pillars by six inches, and worked long, 18-hour shifts during slab concreting days to ensure solid, seamless RCC (reinforced cement concrete) were more than just the achievements. These experiences were not just professional milestones; they were foundational lessons that shaped my approach to problem-solving and leadership in my life's journey.

My decision to pursue civil engineering was more of an accident, driven by the belief that it would secure my family's financial future. However, as I delved deeper into the field, I realized that my potential extended beyond the boundaries of civil engineering.

My thirst for growth and desire to explore new horizons led me to consider a career shift, one that would eventually take me from construction sites to the cutting-edge world of technology - a move inspired by friends in the U.S. who were thriving in the booming IT sector. One friend, in particular, who knew little about me beyond my passion for mathematics, encouraged me to become an AS/400 developer. This advice marked the beginning of a new chapter in my career, during which I would compile over 500 programs with thousands of lines of code during the Y2K phase, ensuring the world didn't come to a standstill at the turn of the millennium.

Throughout my journey, pivotal moments have reinforced my belief in honesty, integrity, and the power of relationships. I vividly remember a time when, during an 8-hour layover in Singapore, I met a client for the first time and ended up signing a contract the very next week. That contract led to an innovation program in Singapore, which became an award-winning project for both me and the client. This experience taught me that the foundation of any successful partnership is trust, built through transparency and genuine intent.

Reflecting back, I find myself extremely fortunate to have met many people and leaders who helped shape my career and became lifelong mentors. These mentors played a critical role in my development, guiding me through challenges, helping me overcome biases, and inspiring me to become a better version of myself. Some of the learnings I share in this book are reflections of the hours-long conversations I had with these mentors, conversations that expanded my thinking and deepened my understanding of leadership and transformation.

Personal challenges have been the cornerstone of my professional journey, shaping not only my career but also my approach to overcoming obstacles. Moving from a small town in Central India (MP) to the bustling National Capital of Delhi in 11th grade was a big leap. The hardest part was switching from my native language (Hindi) to English, the only option for science students in Delhi. With just a few weeks to decide, I made the toughest choice of my life and committed to overcoming this language barrier. The next ten months were a struggle, but I persevered, managing not only to prepare for the most critical year of my academic life but also to conquer the language challenge.

In the 25 years of my technology career, I have managed over 45 engagements across India, Singapore, Australia, and North America, delivering more than 50 large-scale tech solutions. The experiences I've gathered along the way - whether it was navigating the challenges of large complex digital transformation programs, the COVID-19 pandemic, shifting to remote work, or mentoring countless colleagues - have all reinforced my belief in the importance of continuous learning and sharing knowledge. I've always found immense joy in helping others avoid the mistakes I've learned from, believing that the greatest contribution I can make is to pass on the lessons I've gathered.

The idea for this book, *"Navigating the Challenges of Digital Transformation in the World of AI,"* was seeded during conversations with a group of professionals who approached me for guidance on their digital transformation challenges, specially Fixed Bid complex programs. Over the past three years, that seed has grown into a comprehensive guide, drawing on my experiences in managing digital assets from conception to retirement, aligning business, digital, and technology stakeholders, and navigating the complexities of commercial models and their executions.

Change is the only constant, and it's a reality that many dread, especially in the context of digital transformation programs. My hope is that the lessons, anecdotes, and insights shared in this book will help readers become more aware of this intrinsic quality and learn how to navigate it effectively. This book is the culmination of three decades of learning, growth, and a desire to help others succeed in the ever-evolving world of digital transformation.

Disclaimer - this book includes several case-lets, examples, and insights drawn from my professional experience working with various organizations. To respect confidentiality and maintain professional integrity, all case studies have been anonymized, and identifying details have been altered. Any resemblance to specific individuals, companies, or projects is purely coincidental. The intent of these examples is to illustrate key concepts and lessons, not to disclose proprietary or sensitive information.

Who should read this book?

This book is primarily intended as a guide for practitioners and working professionals in the technology industry who have closely experienced the working of software development processes.

If you are a business analyst, project manager, engagement lead, client partner, delivery partner, tech architect, developer, or quality analyst, chances are you will likely find much of the content relevant and relatable to your everyday work. On the enterprise side, whether you are part of a start-up, scale-up, or large enterprise and play a stakeholder role representing clients such as product owner, engineering manager, business system analyst, business and tech sponsor in any digital transformation program, this book may help unravel some of the hidden myths you carry and assist you in navigating common challenges. The language and tone have been kept simple, and a storytelling format has been used as much as possible to minimize cognitive load. Visuals are included to build connections and enhance memory references while reading.

How is the book flow designed?

Welcome!

I understand that reading a book from start to finish in one go is a rare feat, especially with the sheer volume of content we're exposed to daily. It can be challenging to retain and build on the information you consume as you make your way through the chapters.

So, let me ease that journey by offering you a visual reference - a mental model if you will. Imagine this book as a house. We won't just build it all at once; instead, we'll construct it gradually as you explore each chapter.

Each chapter will be like a section or element of this house. Some elements will provide the foundation or pillars, giving you the structural support to understand the basics. Others will be more like the walls, flooring, rooms, roof, and attic - adding details, textures, and depth to your understanding. By the time you finish, you'll have a complete structure and a well-rounded view of digital transformation in the world of changing complexities, built step by step.

As you move through this book, visualize how each piece fits into the larger picture. This approach will not only make the reading experience more engaging but also help you retain and apply the knowledge long after you've turned the last page.

So, let's start building this house together, one brick-or, rather, one chapter-at a time.

Visualize this

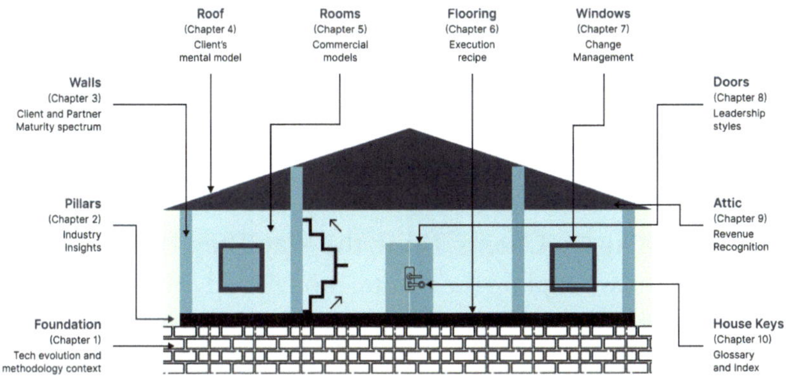

Diagram 1: Mental Model of the Book

Chapter 1: The Fast-Evolving World of Digital Transformation (Foundation) This chapter sets the foundation by exploring the technological advances of the past 30 years and how software development methodologies have evolved. Just as a solid foundation is crucial for a house, understanding these advancements is essential for grounding the discussion on digital transformation. From the days of monolithic mainframes to today's agile and AI-driven approaches, this chapter provides a historical context that helps create a foundational framework for the discussions on digital transformation that follow.

Chapter 2: Industry Leaders' Perspectives - Insights from Leadership Survey (Pillars) Drawing on insights from a comprehensive survey of industry leaders, this chapter forms the pillars of our discussion. It shares insights from a comprehensive survey and interviews with industry practitioners and leaders.

The data collected reflects the collective wisdom of a statistically significant group of professionals, offering a glimpse into the common challenges and priorities in the tech industry.

Chapter 3: Understanding Client and Tech Partner Maturity Spectrum (Walls) This chapter builds the walls of our digital transformation structure by examining the maturity spectrum of clients and tech partners. It provides insights into how organizations can assess their own maturity and evaluate potential partners, shaping the boundaries and capabilities of their transformation effort.

Chapter 4: Why Do Clients Think the Way They Think? (Roofs) In this chapter, we explore the mental models and decision-making processes of key stakeholders. Understanding these "roofs" helps us see how decisions are made and protected during transformation initiatives, offering insights into different approaches, such as "Done is Better than Perfect" and "First Time Right," and how these philosophies influence project execution.

Chapter 5: Exploring Commercial Models in Digital Transformation (Rooms) This chapter delves into the various commercial models that act as the rooms within our digital transformation house. Each model, from Fixed Bid to Outcome-Based, influences how the project space is organized and utilized. The chapter covers the benefits and challenges of each approach, dispels common myths about Fixed Bid programs, and provides practical advice for selecting the right commercial arrangement based on project needs.

Chapter 6: Executing Digital Transformation within Constraints (Flooring) Providing a practical blueprint for execution, this chapter lays the flooring for successful digital transformation programs. It includes strategies for managing budget, time, and scope constraints, and explores various tools and techniques in enhancing efficiency and effectiveness of digital asset development.

Chapter 7: The Art and Science of Change Management (Windows) Change management opens the windows to fresh ideas and effective strategies. This chapter examines why we resist change and introduces models and strategies for operationalizing change to ensure it is embraced and managed effectively within organizations.

Chapter 8: Leadership Styles for Large-Scale Transformation (Doors) Leadership traits and styles open the doors to successful digital transformation. This chapter draws on experiences with various leaders to highlight the key traits needed for effectively navigating large-scale transformations and offers advice on developing these traits within your organization.

Chapter 9: Bonus Chapter - Revenue Recognition in Transformation Programs (Attic) The bonus chapter, akin to the attic, offers additional insights into revenue recognition within transformation programs. It includes engagement simulations to illustrate the effective management of revenue recognition, ensuring compliance and financial transparency.

Chapter 10: Glossary and Index (House Keys) The final chapter provides a comprehensive glossary and index, serving as the house keys. It helps readers navigate the concepts, tools, and methodologies discussed throughout the book, making it easier to access and apply the knowledge.

About the Author

Diljeet Singh Saluja has built a meaningful career in technology and digital transformation, driven by a commitment to experimentation, leadership, and client success. Currently, a Principal Consultant and Delivery Partner at **Thoughtworks** - a global technology consultancy known for its innovative approach to software development using ***Design, Engineering and AI*** - Diljeet leads deliveries for North American clients, bringing together distributed teams to achieve strong outcomes. His experience in workshops on Fixed Bid and transformation projects, combined with a thoughtful approach to risk governance, has made him a 'Go-To' person within the organization.

Before joining Thoughtworks, he served as the Chief Delivery Officer at **Decimal Technologies** - a leading Tech-Fin organization in India that offers technology solutions enabling financial institutions to rapidly expand their businesses - where he helped build and scale the delivery organization significantly and introduced an OKR-driven performance assessment process. His leadership contributed effectively to align the delivery capabilities with the company's growth, enhancing both revenue and client satisfaction.

As the Corporate Vice President and Head of Digital Solutions at **Max Life Insurance** - one of the top three private life insurers in India - Diljeet was hired to build digital capabilities as part of their IT team. He played a key role in promoting agility within the Digital Centre of Excellence and led the development of the

"NEO" customer-facing digital asset, which utilized advanced technologies to improve user experience and partner integration.

During nearly a decade at **SapientNitro** - a global marketing and technology services firm - he held various roles, including Director and Engagement Lead, where he led major digital transformation engagements for multinational clients across India and APAC. His efforts included building content capabilities for globally distributed delivery and developing a client footprint in the Indian market.

Diljeet began his IT journey in the captive technology department of one of the largest car dealerships in the Middle East (SBG), where he took on roles ranging from lead developer to business analyst in AS/400 technology.

Earlier in his career, Diljeet's civil engineering journey began at a Maldivian construction company in Malé, where he was responsible for managing the completion of the superstructure of a 12-story ship-shaped building for the Maldives Ports Authority (MPA).

Diljeet has been greatly influenced by mentors and leaders throughout his career, who have helped shape his approach to leadership and continuous learning. His passion for mentoring and coaching has been constant, as he shares his experiences to help others grow and succeed.

In *"Navigating the Challenges of Digital Transformation in the World of AI,"* Diljeet draws on decades of experience to provide insights into the challenges and opportunities that IT professionals are facing today. Covering topics from the evolution of technologies to the complexities of commercial models, his perspective aims to guide readers through the intricacies of digital transformation in the rapidly evolving world of AI.

Contents – Chapters outline

1. The fast-evolving world of Digital Transformation
   - 1.1. The evolution of technologies
   - 1.2. Methodologies keeping pace with Tech Advances
2. Industry Leaders' Perspectives - Insights from Leadership Survey
3. Understanding Client and tech partner's maturity spectrum
   - 3.1. Client's maturity spectrum
   - 3.2. Partner's maturity spectrum
   - 3.3. Criteria for partner's evaluation
4. Why do clients think the way they think?
   - 4.1. Who are these decision-makers and influencers
   - 4.2. Unique mental models of key decision-makers
   - 4.3. Iterate (Done is Better than Perfect) or First Time Right (FTR)?
5. Exploring commercial models in the Digital Transformation?
   - 5.1. Common commercial models?
   - 5.2. The variants of Fixed Bid models
   - 5.3. Outcome-based commercial models
   - 5.4. Common myths about Fixed Bid programs
6. Executing Digital Transformation programs with Constraints
   - 6.1. Winning recipe for a large transformation program

6.2. How to set an engagement up for success!
6.3. Potential Role of AI & GenAI in the complex execution

7. The Art and Science of 'Change Management'
   7.1. Why do we resist 'Change'
   7.2. Model to deal with 'Change'
   7.3. How to operationalize the 'Change'

8. Leadership styles for a large transformation
   8.1. Leadership traits for a large transformation
   8.2. How to develop these leadership traits

9. Bonus chapter
   9.1. Criteria for Revenue Recognition
   9.2. Engagement Simulations for Revenue Recognition

10. Glossary and Index
   10.1. Glossary
   10.2. Index for Tools and Diagrams

Chapter 1

The fast-evolving world of Digital Transformation

Diagram 2: The fast-evolving world of Digtial Trasnformation

The computing power you carry in your pocket today was once enough to send a man to the moon. Imagine a world where entire businesses were run on machines the size of a room, where the hum of a mainframe was the heartbeat of an enterprise. This was the dawn of information technology - a time when technology began to reshape how organizations operated, laying the groundwork for the incredible advancements we see today.

For many, this might seem like a distant memory from the annals of tech history, but for me, it was a defining moment. My first developer assignment came just a month before the world braced for Y2K.

Picture this:

150 AS/400 developers, all crammed into a room buzzing with the hum of iSeries servers - massive IBM midrange machines with environments ranging from Development to Production. Each of us was handed the Herculean task of combing through millions of lines of RPG/400 code, meticulously altering date variables from 6 digits to 8 (DDMMYY to DDMMYYYY). There was no Ctrl+F to save us; every change had to be made manually and compiled in sequence.

Our mission?

To ensure that, as the clock struck midnight on January 1, 2000, life as we knew it would carry on without a hitch.

1.1 The Evolution of Technologies

The transformation began with **mainframes**, the colossal machines that powered the first wave of enterprise computing. Mainframes were the backbone of large organizations, processing vast amounts of data and performing complex calculations. They were characterized by their reliability, security, and centralized computing power. Despite their advantages, mainframes had a few limitations: they were expensive to maintain, required specialized skills, and offered limited flexibility. The user interface was often limited to text-based terminals, making them less user-friendly than modern systems. As technology evolved, midrange systems emerged to offer a balance of power and cost-effectiveness. They were used in various industries - from, manufacturing and airlines to travel and healthcare to handle specific applications and workloads.

Midrange systems (a.k.a AS/400 machines) played a crucial role in the transition from centralized computing to more distributed and accessible systems. Did you ever notice the airline reservation systems (Galileo, Sabre, and Amadeus) and the green screens?

Those were AS/400 midrange machines. Some of them are still operational and are being modernized slowly.

The advent of **personal computers (PCs)** marked a significant shift in the technological landscape. PCs democratized computing by making it accessible to individuals and small businesses. This shift was fueled by advancements in microprocessors, which enabled powerful yet affordable computing devices. PCs brought about a wave of innovation, from graphical user interfaces (GUIs) to the development of software applications that catered to a wide range of needs. The proliferation of PCs laid the foundation for the interconnected world we live in today.

The **Internet** revolutionized how we communicate, collaborate, and conduct business. The widespread adoption of the Internet in the 1990s and early 2000s transformed the digital landscape, enabling the rise of e-commerce, social media, and cloud computing. The Internet facilitated the development of web-based applications, which provided a new level of accessibility and scalability. Businesses could now reach global audiences, and information could be shared instantaneously.

Then came the era of **smartphones and tablets,** which brought computing power to the palm of our hands. **Mobile computing** revolutionized how we interact with technology, enabling us to stay connected and productive on the go. The development of mobile apps opened up new possibilities for communication, entertainment, and productivity. Mobile computing also spurred the growth of the Internet of Things (IoT). This interconnectedness has led to smart homes, wearable technology, and innovative solutions in various industries.

And then **cloud computing** emerged as a game-changer, offering scalable and cost-effective solutions for data storage, processing, and application deployment. The cloud eliminated the need for businesses to maintain their physical infrastructure, allowing them to focus on innovation and growth. Cloud-based services, such as Software as a Service (SaaS), Platform as a Service (PaaS), and Infrastructure as a Service (IaaS), have become essential components of modern IT strategies.

The explosion of data generated by digital footprints led to the rise of **big data and analytics**. Organizations began to realize the value of harnessing large datasets to gain insights and make informed decisions. Big data technologies, such as Hadoop and Spark, enable the processing and analysis of massive amounts of data in real-time. Analytics has become a cornerstone of business intelligence, helping organizations understand customer behavior, optimize operations, and identify new opportunities.

The **2020 pandemic** has greatly accelerated the adoption of digital technology for both individual consumers (B2C) and businesses (B2B). For everyday customers, the need to shop, work, and access services from home led to a significant increase in the use of online platforms like e-commerce, telehealth, and streaming services. People who were once unsure about using digital tools now depend on them for daily activities, and this change is likely to persist.

For businesses, the pandemic forced a rapid shift to digital solutions to maintain operations running while dealing with lockdowns and social distancing. Companies had to adopt online tools for communication, collaboration, and conducting business, which also changed how they work with clients and partners.

The pandemic pushed everyone, both individuals and businesses, to adopt digital technology faster than expected. This rapid change has made digital strategies more important than ever for staying competitive and growing in the future.

Now, **Artificial intelligence (AI)** has arrived to revolutionize technology, transforming how we interact with machines and make decisions. AI encompasses a wide range of technologies, including machine learning (ML), natural language processing (NLP), computer vision, and robotics. AI-powered systems can analyze data, recognize patterns, and make predictions with unprecedented accuracy and speed. They can automate tasks, provide personalized recommendations, and even drive autonomous vehicles (AV). AI has the potential to revolutionize industries, from healthcare to finance, by augmenting human capabilities and unlocking new possibilities.

1.2 Methodologies Keeping Pace with Tech Advances

As technology has evolved, so have the methodologies used to develop and implement these technologies. The evolution of development methodologies has been crucial in harnessing the power of new technological advancements and ensuring their successful integration into businesses and everyday life.

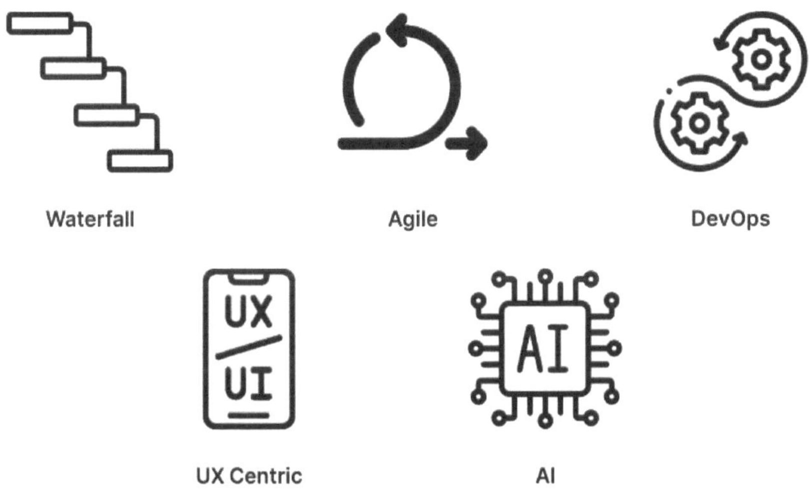

Diagram 3: Development Methodologies

Waterfall Methodologies: The Early Days

In the **early days of mainframes and midrange machines**, the predominant development methodology was linear and sequential, also known as Waterfall methodology. **Inspired by civil engineering and large construction** work, where the master plan, layouts, and detailed designs are prepared and approved before the construction begins, this method involves distinct phases of a project such as requirements gathering, design completion, implementation, testing, deployment, and maintenance. Each phase has to be completed before moving on to the next, making it appear to be a relatively rigid but straightforward process. While suitable for projects with well-defined requirements and low uncertainty, the Waterfall method struggled to accommodate changes once the project was underway. This limitation became increasingly apparent as technology began to evolve rapidly and projects grew in complexity.

"Some people say the Waterfall methodology is a thing of the past. Would you agree?"

Agile Methodology: Embracing Flexibility

With the **advent of personal computers and the internet**, the **need for a more flexible and iterative approach** to development became evident. The Agile methodology emerged as a response to this need, emphasizing collaboration, customer feedback, and incremental delivery.

Agile methodologies allow development teams to work in short cycles called sprints, where they continuously prioritize and reassess their work. This approach enables teams to adapt to changes more effectively and deliver working software more frequently. Agile's focus on collaboration and customer feedback has made it a popular choice for projects that require adaptability and a swift response to changing requirements. **Inspired by manufacturing practices**, Agile evolved into Lean Agile, which emphasizes **eliminating waste**, optimizing processes, and delivering value to customers quickly. Lean principles have been adapted to software development to improve efficiency and reduce time-to-market.

"What is the adoption rate of Agile methodologies despite its popularity?

Something we can ponder upon! I will provide some color to this debatable topic in one of the chapters called 'Common myths'.

DevOps: Bridging Development and Operations

As cloud computing and continuous delivery became more prevalent, the need to bridge the gap between development and operations teams **gave birth to DevOps**. It focuses on automating and streamlining the entire software delivery process, from code development to deployment and maintenance.

By promoting collaboration between developers and IT operations, DevOps aims to shorten development cycles, increase deployment frequency, and ensure more reliable releases, often known as **DORA metrics**. This approach has become essential in a world where businesses need to rapidly deploy updates and maintain high levels of system availability.

"What's the adoption of DevOps in the technology industry despite its game-changing impact?

I will share some interesting anecdotes about this in the 'winning recipe' chapter of this book.

UX: Enhancing User Experience in Digital Products

While DevOps was transforming software development by speeding up the process and reducing the time it takes to get a product to market, User Experience (UX) design was focusing on ensuring that the user's experience was front and center. UX design emerged as a vital discipline when companies realized that technology isn't just about functionality—it's about how users feel when they interact with a product. By putting the user's needs and preferences at the center, UX design aims to enhance the overall experience, ensuring that digital products are intuitive, accessible, and satisfying.

This approach goes beyond aesthetics; it involves understanding user behavior, conducting research, and testing designs to create seamless interactions. In a digital world where user satisfaction can make or break a product, UX design has become a cornerstone of product development, ensuring that the end result resonates with users and meets their expectations.

"What percentage of the technology population understands the real difference between UI and UX? Between wireframes and visual designs, which one requires more application of science versus art?"

Stay tuned; you will get some insights on this as well in this book.

The Role of AI in Development Methodologies

As the digital landscape continues to evolve, the integration of AI into development practices is becoming inevitable. It's not just about automation anymore; it's about empowering systems with the ability to think, learn, and adapt on their own.

Artificial intelligence is not only a transformative technology but also an enabler of advanced development methodologies. AI and machine learning algorithms can analyze vast amounts of data to identify patterns, predict outcomes, and optimize processes. This capability has the potential to be integrated into various stages of the development lifecycle, from requirements gathering to testing and maintenance.

Many AI-driven tools (such as Pieces, Tebnine, OpenAI Codex, Code Whisperer, Github Copilot etc.) are being experimented with to **automate repetitive tasks during the development process, enhance code quality through intelligent code reviews, and provide insights for better decision-making**.

"Can AI really make developers' lives easier and make them more productive? Do you think AI-produced code will be secure and ready to put into production easily?"

This is understandably in a "wait-and-see" stage, as the impact of AI on development is evolving rapidly.

As developers gain more experience with AI tools, we'll likely get a clearer sense of the technology's strengths and limitations, especially regarding secure, production-ready code. So, for now, we're in an exciting period of experimentation, discovering AI's capabilities and constraints, and building an understanding of how it can be best applied in the software development lifecycle.

Chapter 2

Industry Leaders' Perspectives - Insights from Leadership Survey

Many aspects of digital transformation that we often contemplate seek validation from our peers and that's natural. As social beings, we rely on social proof for reassurance. This chapter uncovers answers to common questions you might have and reveals what a statistically significant group of leaders are thinking, providing clarity and confidence in your own approach.

First, let me outline the number of people and the personas I reached out to for this survey, along with the questions asked. This will provide context for the insights shared and help you understand the perspectives that shaped the results.

The people I have chosen for this survey are digital transformation leaders and practitioners who have 15 plus years' experience in technology, product domain and transformation program management. As per latest **McKinsey and Deloitte report**, 15% of IT industry represents this cohort.

With an 85% confidence level and a ±10% margin of error, the statistically significant sample size for a survey is 27 (**as per survey sample sizing calculator**) . Keeping this in mind, I reached out to 40 individuals within my network in LinkedIn, all of whom hold mid and senior leadership positions across various organizations, both in IT services and product companies. After receiving 30 valid responses, I concluded the survey, ensuring a representative view of this leadership segment.

The questions asked in the survey were as follows:

1. What has been the most significant benefit your organization has experienced from digital transformation efforts? (multi select response enabled)

    A. Improved operational efficiency
    B. Enhanced customer experience
    C. Accelerated innovation
    D. Cost savings
    E. Others

2. As an Enterprise, what criteria do you use to evaluate the maturity of your tech partners in supporting your digital transformation efforts? (multi select response enabled)

    A. Technical expertise
    B. Price value proposition
    C. Past performance and reliability
    D. Delivery and execution capabilities
    E. Others

3. Who are the key decision-makers in your organization's digital transformation initiatives, and how do they influence the process? (multi select response enabled)

    A. C-suite executives (CEO, CDO, CIO, etc.)
    B. Department heads and managers
    C. External consultants and advisors
    D. Cross-functional teams
    E. Others

4. As an Enterprise, what has been your experience with different commercial models (e.g. Fixed Bid, T&M, Outcome Based) in different transformation projects?

Long text response enabled

5. As Tech service partners, what have been the most commonly used commercial models as part of your service offering?

   A. Fixed Bid Model

   B. T&M model

   C. Cost Plus Fee

   D. Outcome-based model

   E. Others

6. If you selected T&M in Q5, what challenges do you typically encounter during program execution?

   A. Delivering the expected value within the expected budget

   B. Delivering the expected value within the given timeframe

   C. Delivering the full scope within the allocated budget

   D. Others

7. How do you ensure that your commercial agreements align with the desired outcomes of your digital transformation efforts?

   Long text response enabled

8. What leadership qualities are most critical for driving successful digital transformation initiatives?

   Long text response enabled

9. How do you view the role of AI in the digital transformation initiatives? (mult select response enabled)

   A. As a critical enabler of innovation

   B. As a tool for cost reduction

   C. As a way to enhance customer experience

   D. As a potential risk due to ethical concerns

   E. Others

Let me start with the survey responses and the key insights that emerged.

Response to "**Question 1 - What has been the most significant benefit your organization has experienced from digital transformation efforts?**" was quite interesting. Approximately 50% of respondents indicated that the most significant benefit their organizations experienced from digital transformation was enhanced customer experience, closely followed by improved operational efficiency.

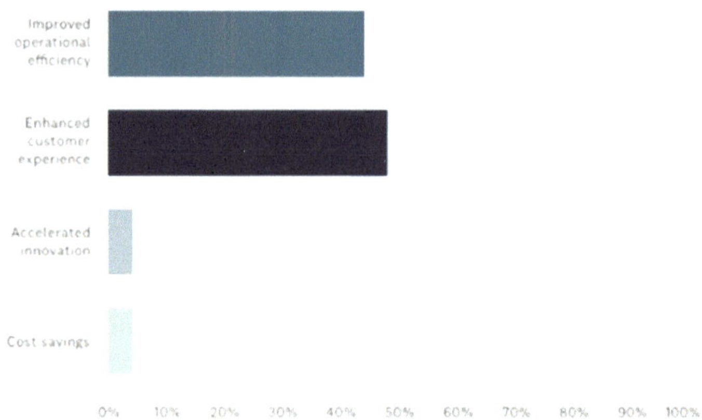

ANSWER CHOICES	RESPONSES
Improved operational efficiency	44.00%
Enhanced customer experience	48.00%
Accelerated innovation	4.00%
Cost savings	4.00%
TOTAL	

Diagram 4: Survey Response - Q1

This insight reinforces the growing importance of customer centricity in today's business landscape. Whether the focus is on external or internal customers, the ability to align business models and processes around customer needs continues to be a critical success factor. Digital technologies are at the forefront of enabling this transformation, allowing organizations to enhance customer experiences and improve efficiency. Companies that fail to adopt this customer-first mindset risk becoming obsolete or marginalized, as the business world continues to prioritize customer value and adaptability.

I have often heard from CXOs in my network about the challenge of selecting the right partner to accelerate their digital transformation. In a highly competitive space where numerous tech consulting and service firms are vying for a piece of the enterprise IT budget, making the right choice can be daunting. Businesses have to carefully evaluate potential partners amidst all the noise.

When asked about the key factors businesses consider "**Question 2 - As an Enterprise, what criteria do you use to evaluate the maturity of your tech partners in supporting your digital transformation efforts?**" while selecting a tech partner, many leaders highlighted that among various parameters, delivery and execution capabilities consistently come out on top.

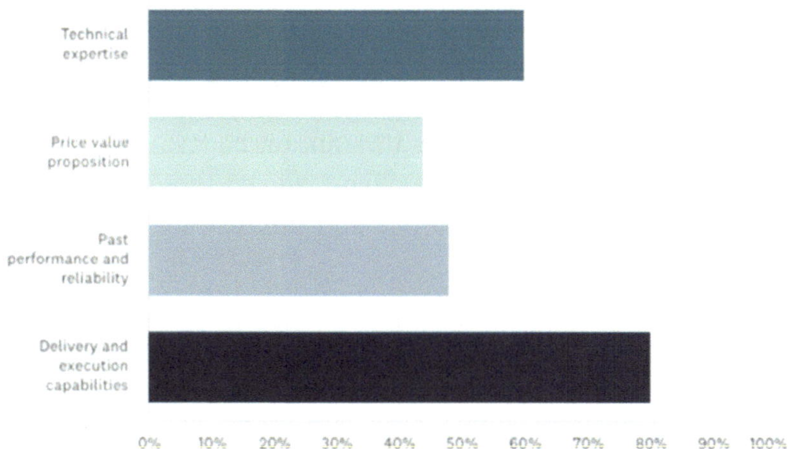

Diagram 5: Survey Response - Q2

It's not enough to be swayed by a polished technical presentation or to choose the partner offering the lowest quote. What enterprises truly need is proof of a partner's digital transformation expertise, demonstrated through strong delivery and execution track records. Leaders recommend looking for alignment in ways of working and ensuring the partner understands the complexity of the organization's ecosystem. Critical factors include whether the partner has made accurate assumptions, recognized risks, and proposed a solid risk mitigation strategy. This feedback strongly influenced the focus on a "winning recipe" for successful partnerships, which I delve into further in Chapter 6 of this book.

A common question "(**Question 3 - Who are the key decision-makers in your organization's digital transformation initiatives?**" from partner teams is about identifying the key decision-makers when selecting tech partners.

It was quite evident from the survey responses that leaders believe that department heads and managers may have some influence, especially in new logo acquisitions, they rarely hold the final decision-making power. For more efficient results, tech partners should focus on engaging with senior leadership, such as CIOs, CTOs, BU heads or decision-makers within the C-suite, who are more likely to make strategic partnership choices. If a digital transformation effort involves a significant budget or is pivotal to gaining a competitive edge, it often lands on these CXOs' desks. This can shorten the sales cycle and improve the likelihood of conversion.

Around 80% of industry leaders agree that influencing this CXO group is the key to winning partnerships. Engaging at this level ensures alignment with strategic goals and speeds up the decision-making process.

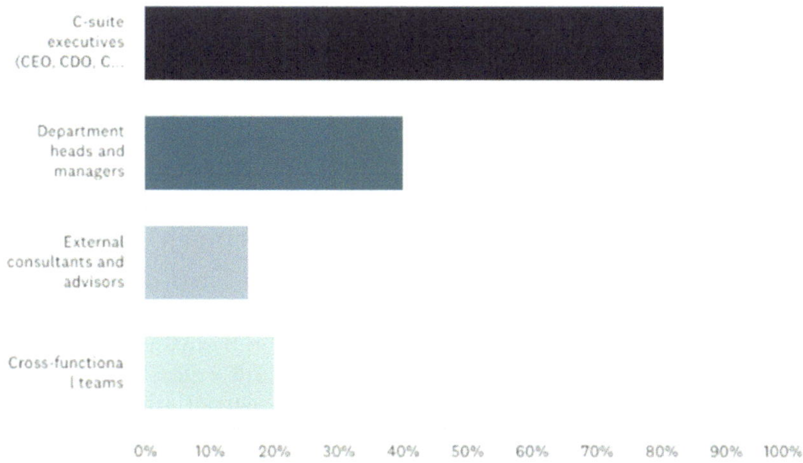

Diagram 6: Survey Response - Q3

Now the most difficult decisions for an **enterprise (businesses)** when getting ready to begin a digital transformation initiative. "**Question 4 - Which commercial models they should go with?**" Some of the options provided as part of this question were:

1. T&M (time and material)

2. Fixed Bid

3. Outcome based

4. Any other

Since the question was subjective, the responses gathered were not straightforward and required more in-depth explanations. I was pleasantly surprised to see the thoughtfulness and details many respondents provided in their answers. To make this easier for my readers to digest, I will summarize the key insights from these responses.

From the survey responses, it's clear that:

While outcome-based models are ideal, they often remain aspirational due to the high-risk appetite and transparent communication required.

Fixed Bid is favoured as it brings predictability and aligns the partner with delivering agreed-upon scope within budget.

Meanwhile, T&M is still popular, especially in environments that are either exploratory or require frequent iterations and flexibility.

Many respondents highlighted that the maturity of an organization plays a key role in the selection. Enterprises with a dedicated team driving the transformation tend to have more success with fixed bid or outcome-based models. For others, a bimodal approach, which blends Fixed Bid and T&M, is often seen as the most pragmatic option.

In conclusion, the commercial model decision is complex and context-dependent. A detailed exploration of these models and their pros and cons is further discussed in an entire chapter dedicated to this topic.

On the other hand, when I asked **service providers (tech partners)** "**Question 5 - about their preferred commercial models**", it was no surprise that T&M (Time & Material) topped the list with 60% preferring it, which makes sense given its lower risk for the partner. However, I was intrigued to see that Fixed Bid models are gradually gaining traction, with 40% of tech partners now favouring it.

This shift signals a growing willingness to share risk and a potential increase in trust between partners and clients.

The conflicting perceptions between enterprises favouring the Fixed Bid model and tech partners preferring the Time and Materials (T&M) model can be attributed to several factors, reflecting the differing priorities and risk tolerances of each stakeholder group.

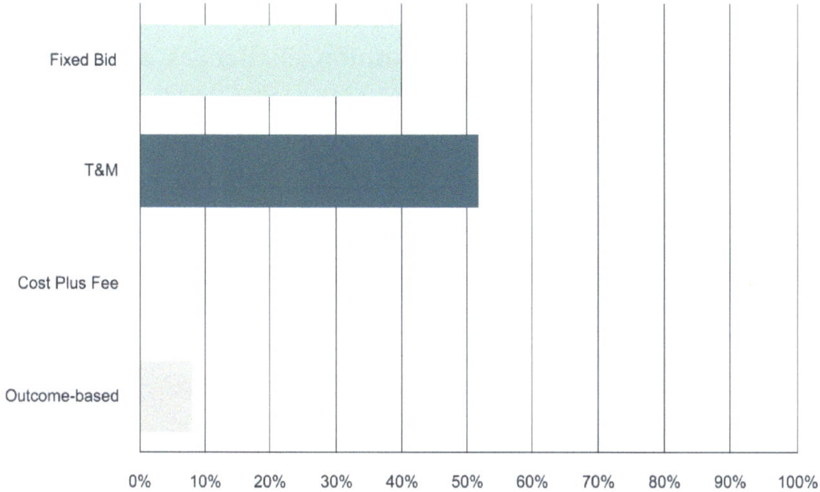

Diagram 7: Survey Response - Q5

Let me add my point of view here.

While tech partners view T&M as a less risky approach, allowing for flexibility in billing based on graded rate cards and varying skill sets, enterprises have a different outlook.

Enterprises prioritize value for their investment. Regardless of the commercial model chosen by them, they expect to achieve tangible results. Many enterprise CTOs and CIOs operate under tight deadlines for their Minimum Viable Product (MVP) launches, with predetermined scopes. In such scenarios, even with a T&M agreement, Enterprises are looking for defintive outcomes within a given timeline and budget and tech partners are not left with any choice then to absorb unforeseen risks and additional costs associated with delays or scope creep to meet client expectations.

This situation illustrates the complexities of project management in general. Even if it's a T&M engagement, the burden of managing risks often falls on the tech partners, despite the perception of lower risk associated with the model.

This leads us to a more profound inquiry for tech partners: **"Question 6- what are the common challenges encountered during the execution of Time and Materials (T&M) programs?"** The answers to this question have been quite clear.

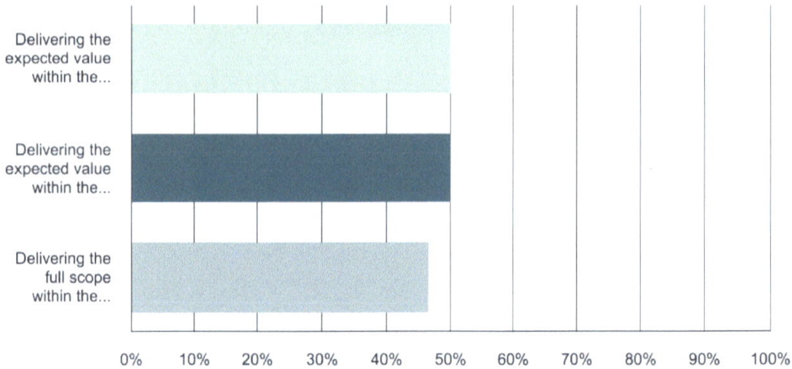

ANSWER CHOICES	RESPONSES
Delivering the expected value within the budget	50.00%
Delivering the expected value within the given timeframe	50.00%
Delivering the full scope within the allocated budget	37.50%

Diagram 8: Survey Response - Q6

Delivering the expected value within the allocated budget (50%), followed by expected value within the given timeframe (50%) and full scope within the allocated budget (appx 40%).

The biggest challenge for delivery team (despite the engagement being T&M) is same as it would be for Fixed Bid engagements.

So why this contrarian view about T&M engagements?

I spoke to many sales and delivery leaders to double click on this aspect of T&M engagements. In my opinion, this contrarian view is coming from how T&M is being sold versus how it is being delivered. Imagine Tech partner's Sales team who are selling the deals. They prefer T&M because it's easy to sell on rate cards. For the same team sizing a deal for fixed bid will needs a pursuit team to conduct a due diligence, understand the complexity and risks behind the initiative and estimate the effort accordingly. That's a huge effort and longer sales cycle. Hence the sales team 's first choice is T&M whereas delivery team's struggle remains same (the above response).

In fact, this is the very thought that pushes enterprise teams to favour Fixed Bid models and often choose the RFP route with a large transformation initiative.

This insight led me to believe that tech partners need to know the winning recipe to manage a complex digital transformation program and know the nuances of how to operate within constraints (of budget, scope and timeline) regardless of the commercial model signed between two parties.

And it's not a simple feat by any means.

This lands us to next question "**Question 7 - What does both parties THINK on how to align their program success with various commercial models**"

Let me bring up a few subjective statements from survey respondents to share their sentiments.

"Foremost the outcomes are objectified"

"Commercial agreements should be built ground up- from the desired outcome of the program. Outcome leads to efforts and efforts lead to commercial agreements"

"Detailed scope and discovery at the start of the project. Outcome to be clearly defined during discovery."

"Defined KPIs and metrics upfront"

"By defining OKRs and measuring outcomes against them"

"Governance framework"

"Frequent governance and transparency on financial forecasting"

"First engage in discovery engagements and help unveil what all needs to be accomplished for complex initiatives"

"Maximum clarity on deliverables and leadership governance"

"COO office to provide Cross-Functional team and governance"

"Governance and OCM strategy"

They are quite thoughtful response and captures good enough ground of execution. Good news is that most of the respondents align on

1 The importance of objective measures (success metrics of the program)

2 Good discovery for complex programs

3. Governance

This is no surprise - we all know these elements are crucial. But many of us may lack a clear path for navigating them effectively. This book aims to uncover some of the strategies to tackle these execution challenges in any complex program.

The success of transformational programs can also hinge on the leadership styles of those at the helm. I wanted to gather leaders' perspectives on the skills and qualities they value most and would aim to embody, if they were leading these initiatives.

Response to this question **"Question 8 - What leadership qualities are most critical for driving successful digital transformation initiatives?"** were truly insightful. The most frequently mentioned qualities included:

Open communication, empathy, perseverance, inclusive, collaborative

Two additional qualities stood out in the responses:

1. **The ability to make tough decisions** – Leaders must be ready to make critical, sometimes difficult, choices to steer the transformation effectively.
2. **Consistent vision articulation** – Repeatedly communicating the vision throughout the execution phase ensures that teams remain aligned and motivated.

These qualities, along with the previously mentioned traits, shape a well-rounded approach to leading successful digital transformation initiatives.

I am going deeper in the chapter 8 (**leadership styles**) to add more dimensions relevant for them to lead the complex transformation programs.

And the final question, **"Question 9 - How do you view the role of AI in digital transformation initiatives?"** had a more forward-looking perspective, especially amid today's market buzz around AI.

The responses made one thing clear: enterprises are eagerly exploring AI as a means to innovate and create a competitive edge. Leaders expressed that, while the technology is still evolving, its potential to transform business processes and enhance decision-making is undeniable. It's likely that, over the next few decades, we'll all witness AI's transformative effects on both business and everyday life as it integrates deeper into our workflows and strategies.

Having explored the evolving tech landscape and the methodologies that support business growth, let's delve into how clients select their technology partners to drive forward their transformation initiatives.

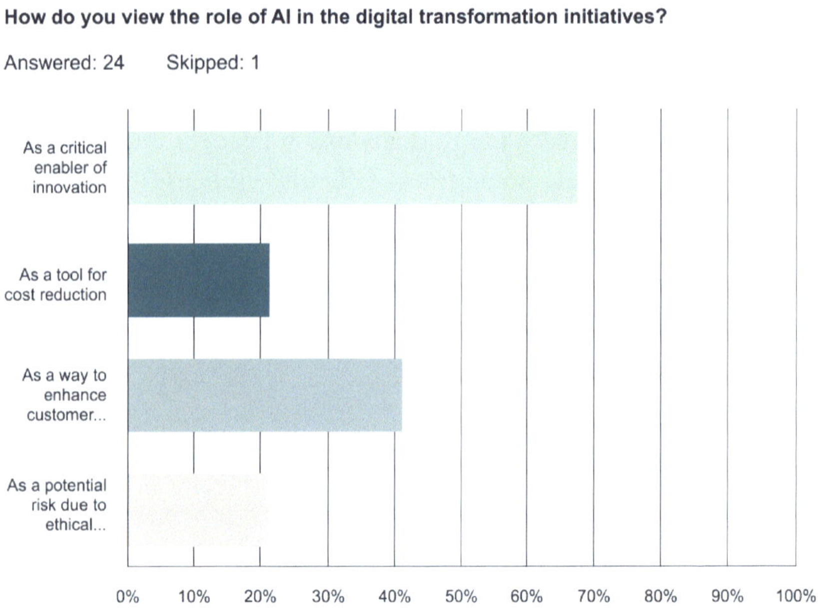

Diagram 9: Survey Response - Q9

Chapter 3

Understanding Client and Tech Partner Maturity Spectrum

Technology is fundamentally reshaping the way businesses operate, driving efficiency, innovation, and growth across industries. What once required human effort and oversight, from routine tasks to complex computations, is now increasingly managed by advanced technological systems. Automation, artificial intelligence, and data analytics are streamlining operations, enabling businesses to focus on strategic decision-making and creative problem-solving.

As technology continues to evolve, both clients and partners have significantly advanced in their understanding and utilization of these tools. They have matured in their ability to harness technology not just as a means of improving efficiency but as a strategic asset that drives competitive advantage. This evolution reflects a deepening appreciation of how technology can be leveraged to enhance productivity, reduce costs, and open new avenues for innovation.

Clients are becoming more sophisticated in their technology demands, seeking solutions that are not only effective but also scalable and adaptable to their changing needs. Meanwhile, partners are evolving their offerings to align with these expectations, delivering more integrated, intelligent, and tailored solutions. This mutual growth in technological maturity is enabling businesses to unlock new potential, paving the way for more agile, responsive, and future-ready operations.

3.1 Client's Maturity Spectrum

Today, businesses of all sizes-small, medium, and large-are leveraging technology to differentiate themselves and deliver greater value to their customers. Let me share my perspective on how their maturity cycle evolves.

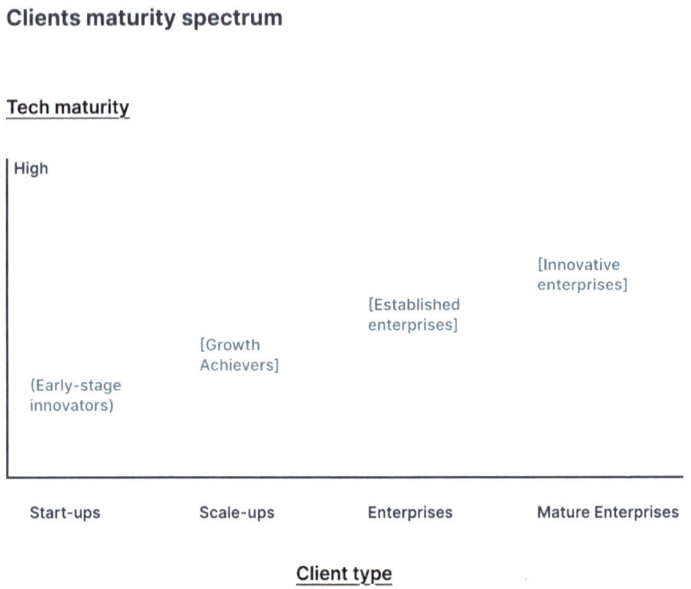

Diagram 10: Client's Maturity Spectrum - A graphical view

Client type	Tech maturity	Attributes	Focus	Needs
Early-stage innovators	Low to medium	Nascent strategies, rapid experimentation	Speed to market, innovative solutions	Scalable solutions, support for rapid development
Growth achievers	Medium	Evolving strategies, growing infrastructure	Scalability, performance, integration	Robust solutions, integration support
Established enterprises	High	Well-defined strategies, complex systems	Stability, risk management, compliance	Advanced solutions, compliance, risk management
Innovative enterprises	Very high	Highly advanced strategies, leading-edge practices	Innovation leadership, strategic advantage	Cutting-edge solutions, thought leadership

Diagram 11: Client's Maturity Spectrum - A tabular view

Early Stage Innovators focus on rapid development and require scalable, flexible solutions. **Growth Achievers** seek robust systems to support their scaling efforts. **Advanced Enterprises** emphasize stability and efficiency, needing solutions that align with their established frameworks. Finally, **Innovative Enterprises** lead the industry with cutting-edge technologies, prioritizing continuous innovation and strategic advantages. Understanding these categories allows tech partners to create and provide for more tailored technology solutions that align with each client's specific needs and maturity level.

And how will AI impact these business segments?

1. **Early Stage Innovators:** AI has the potential to empower these companies to accelerate development and market entry by automating tasks and leveraging data-driven insights. They may use AI for rapid prototyping and predictive analytics, allowing for faster progress with reduced risk.

2. **Growth Achievers:** As they scale, AI might help optimize operations and improve customer experiences. AI-driven analytics may offer insights into customer behavior and market trends, which are essential for managing growth efficiently. AI may also aid them in supply chain optimization and workforce management.

3. **Advanced Enterprises:** AI may enhance the efficiency and stability of enterprises by refining processes and improving decision-making through advanced analytics, provided they already have some level of data platform for the enterprise needs. Predictive maintenance and streamlined operations might further allow these companies to maintain a competitive edge and reduce system downtime.

4. **Innovative Enterprises:** AI may serve as a catalyst for industry leaders, enabling them to drive breakthrough innovations

and redefine standards. They are already engaged in multiple experiments with AI in R&D and real-time data processing to help them maintain their leadership and push industry boundaries.

3.2 Partner' Maturity Spectrum

On the other hand, tech partners are essential in driving business success through technological innovation. By offering cutting-edge expertise in automation, advanced analytics, artificial intelligence, machine learning, and seamless system integration, these tech partners empower businesses to transform their operations, harness data-driven insights, and unlock new levels of efficiency and innovation. Whether they are small startups or large global firms, tech partners enable organizations to leverage the latest technology to gain a competitive edge, optimize performance, and deliver exceptional value to their customers. Based on their size and maturity, tech service providers and partners can generally categorized as follows:

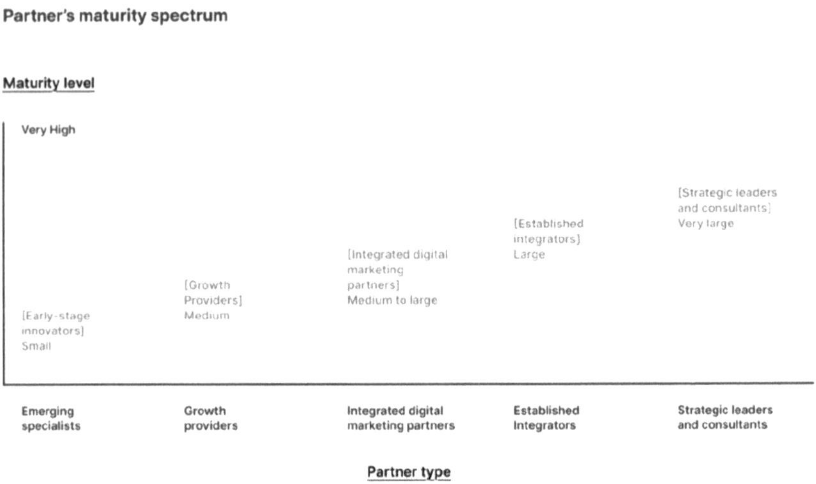

Diagram 12: Partner's Maturity Spectrum - A graphical view

Partner type	Maturity level	Attributes	Focus	Client Fit
Emerging Specialists	*Low to medium*	*Small, niche firms with specialized skills*	*Innovation, agility, specialized services*	*Start-ups or those needing niche, cutting-edge solutions*
Growth providers	*Medium*	*Medium-sized firms expanding capabilities*	*Scaling operations, improved service deliver*	*Scale-ups or mid-sized enterprises needing robust solutions*
Integrated Marketing Partners	*Medium to High*	*Firms combining marketing strategy with technology*	*Brand development, MarTech integration, omnichannel strategy*	*Businesses seeking comprehensive marketing and technology solutions*
Established Integrators	*High*	*Large firms with comprehensive services and track record*	*System integration, process optimization, Legacy modernisation*	*Established enterprises needing scalable platforms, tech transformation*
Strategic Leaders	*Very high*	*Leading global firms with extensive expertise*	*Strategic partnerships, industry-defining solutions, business-technology integration*	*Mature enterprises and governments seeking leadership, innovation, and comprehensive transformation*

Diagram 13: Partner's Maturity Spectrum - A tabular view

How is AI going to shape these partner segments?

1. **Emerging Specialists (Early-Stage Innovators, Small)**: Emerging specialists, often small and nimble, are likely to benefit immensely from AI's ability to automate and streamline processes. AI tools may help them punch above their weight, enabling them to deliver advanced solutions without the extensive resources larger firms possess. However, the challenge will be the rapid adoption and integration of AI technologies, which might require upskilling and investment.

2. **Growth Providers (Medium)**: For growth providers, AI will present an opportunity to scale efficiently. As these partners are typically in a growth phase, AI may help optimize operations, enhance decision-making, and deliver more value to clients. They may focus on integrating AI into existing processes to support rapid expansion and improve client offerings, but they

may also need to invest heavily in AI technologies and skills to stay ahead of competitors.

3. **Integrated Digital Marketing Partners (Medium to Large)**: AI is likely to enable these marketing tech partners to offer more personalized and data-driven marketing solutions. With AI, they may better analyze consumer behavior, optimize campaigns in real-time, and deliver more precise targeting. This should enhance their ability to drive customer engagement and ROI for their clients. However, they will need to continuously evolve their AI capabilities to meet ever-changing market demands.
4. **Established System Integrators (Large)**: Established system integrators (SI) may use AI to further solidify their role in managing complex, large-scale projects. AI might help them automate project management, streamline integration processes, and provide more accurate forecasting and risk management based on their current system capabilities. They are expected to lead in implementing AI solutions for their clients, further strengthening their market position, but may face challenges in adapting their existing infrastructure and workforce to fully integrate AI.
5. **Strategic Leaders and Consultants (Very Large)**: As the most mature and experienced partners, strategic leaders and consultants will harness AI to drive innovation and provide high-level strategic guidance to their clients. AI is likely to enable them to deliver insights based on vast data analysis, helping clients navigate complex business landscapes and stay ahead of trends. For this, they will need to stay on the cutting edge of AI advancements to continue offering new service solutions.

3.3 Criteria for Partner's Evaluation

Having understood the clients' and partners' maturity in the technology landscape, choosing the right technology and implementation partner is a significant challenge for clients, given the complexities of aligning with their business objectives and project needs. This decision involves a detailed evaluation of factors such as the partner's expertise and maturity, their capability to provide innovative solutions, their track record of success, their value proposition, and their compatibility with the client's culture and operational style. Clients may also consider whether the partner can scale and adapt to evolving requirements. A thorough assessment ensures that the selected partner will effectively support the client's goals and contribute to successful program outcomes.

Let's explore some of these parameters in detail.

1. **Alignment with Objectives:** Clients seek partners whose solutions align with both their long-term and short-term objectives. They evaluate whether the provider understands their business goals and can provide technology solutions that support those goals. This alignment ensures that the technology investments contribute to the overall business strategy rather than just merely addressing immediate technical needs.

2. **Problem-Solving Capability:** Clients look for partners who can not only provide technology but also act as problem solvers. They assess the partner's ability to understand unique challenges and propose innovative solutions. This involves evaluating the partner's industry and domain expertise, technical knowledge, and creativity to solve problems.

3. **Technical Expertise:** The technical prowess of a partner is a critical factor. Clients evaluate the partner's expertise in relevant technologies, including their ability to implement and manage these technologies effectively. This assessment often involves reviewing case studies, client testimonials, and the partner's track record in similar projects.

4. **Innovation and Future-Readiness:** Clients want partners who are at the forefront of technological innovation. They look for partners who invest in research and development, stay updated with emerging technologies, and offer forward-thinking solutions. This future-readiness ensures that the client's technology stack remains relevant and competitive in the long run.

5. **Delivery and Execution Capabilities:** A partner's past performance is often seen as a strong indicator of their ability to deliver. Clients examine the partner's portfolio, paying close attention to project success rates, adherence to timelines, and ability to stay within budget. A proven track record provides confidence in the partner's reliability and capability to execute complex projects..

   Clients scrutinize the methodologies and processes that partners employ to discover, analyze, and develop the solution. They look for partners who adopt robust and flexible development methodologies, such as Agile, DevOps, or Lean that can adapt to the client's specific needs. This ensures that the partner can manage the project efficiently and accommodate any changes that may arise during the development lifecycle.

6. **Financial Stability:** The financial stability of a partner is crucial for long-term partnerships. Clients assess the partner's financial health to ensure that they have the resources to sustain the projects, invest in new technologies, and fulfill commitments. A financially stable partner is less likely to face disruptions that could impact the project.

7. **Scalability:** Clients evaluate the partner's ability to scale their services in line with the client's growth. This involves assessing the partner's infrastructure, resource availability, and capacity to manage increased workloads. A scalable partner can support the client's evolving needs without compromising on quality or efficiency.

8. **Cultural Fit:** The cultural alignment between the client and partner is a significant consideration. Clients seek partners whose values, work culture, and communication styles align with their own. A good cultural fit fosters a collaborative and productive working relationship, which is essential for the success of the project.

9. **Communication and Transparency:** Effective communication and transparency are vital for building trust and ensuring smooth project execution. Clients evaluate the partner's communication practices, including their responsiveness, clarity, and willingness to share information. Transparent partners are more likely to foster a strong partnership and address any issues promptly.

10. **Price-Value Proposition**: Clients evaluate the partner's pricing structure to ensure it provides a good balance of cost and value. The focus is on the overall value and return on investment, including both initial implementation costs and long-term operational expenses. Typically, clients create a business case for every initiative where they would want to capture the benefits they would like to derive from the program and compare this against the cost, typically known as TCO (Total Cost of Ownership). Overall, a partner that excels in price-value proposition shows that they can deliver meaningful benefits while aligning with the client's financial expectations. This capability makes them a strong contender in the client's selection process, reflecting positively on their scorecard.

Caselet 1

"Enterprise clients are typically cautious about relying on a single partner for all their needs. When I was responsible for managing a digital applications portfolio on the enterprise side, we were mindful of this. For instance, we partnered with nimble startup

firms for rapid prototyping of agency apps, aiming to create and test new digital journeys tailored to digitally savvy agents. On the other hand, when it came to building a new D2C buying platform, we issued an RFP to the top five tier-1 partners. We selected one based on their delivery execution expertise, scalable solution, and proposed commercial model. After a few collaborative workshops, we agreed on a Fixed-Fee-cum-Outcome-Based (70-30) model."

Chapter 4

Why do clients think the way they do?

The evaluation of technology partners often involves a diverse group of decision-makers, each focusing on different aspects of the partnership. While CIOs, CTOs, CDOs, and BU heads typically lead technical assessments, CEOs, CFOs, COOs, CMOs, and other stakeholders provide strategic, business, financial, and legal perspectives. Decision makers and influencers may also differ based on the scale and the organizational structure of the business.

4.1 Who are the decision makers and influencers?

Let's look at who the decision makers and influencers are in the client ecosystem when it comes to choosing the right technology partner for their key transformation program.

Chief Executive Officer (CEO)

- **Business Strategy**: The CEO provides overall strategic direction and ensures that any technology investments align with the organization's broader business goals and vision. They are often involved in final decisions, especially for high-impact or high-cost partnerships.
- **Business Outcomes**: The CEO is concerned with how the technology partner will affect the organization's competitive position, market strategy, and long-term success.
- **Approval Authority**: The CEO's approval may be required for major decisions involving significant investments or strategic shifts.

Chief Marketing Officer (CMO)

- **Marketing Strategy**: The CMO considers how the partner's technology aligns with marketing (including digital marketing) strategies and capabilities, such as data analytics, CRM systems, and marketing automation tools.
- **Customer Experience**: The CMO evaluates how the technology partner's solutions can enhance customer engagement, marketing effectiveness, and the overall brand experience.
- **Innovation and Branding**: The CMO may also consider how innovative technology solutions can help differentiate the company's brand and improve marketing initiatives.

Chief Operating Officer (COO)

- **Operational Efficiency:** Assesses how the technology partner's solutions enhance business processes and operational efficiency.
- **Business Impact:** Evaluates the effect of the solutions on daily operations and alignment with operational goals.
- **Performance Monitoring:** Ensures the technology meets operational expectations and supports business objectives.

Chief Information Officer (CIO)

- **Strategic Alignment**: Ensures that the technology partner's solutions align with the organization's IT strategy and overall business objectives.
- **Technical Evaluation**: Assesses the technical capabilities, integration possibilities, and fit of the partner's solutions within the existing IT infrastructure.
- **Implementation Oversight**: Oversees how the technology will be integrated and managed, including evaluating support and maintenance services.

Chief Digital Officer (CDO)

- **Digital Transformation**: Evaluates how the technology partner can drive digital innovation and enhance digital capabilities within the organization.
- **User Experience**: Assesses the impact of the technology on customer and user experience, ensuring alignment with digital strategy and goals.
- **Innovation**: Focuses on how the partner's solutions contribute to advancing the organization's digital transformation and staying ahead of market trends.

Chief Financial Officer (CFO)

- **Cost-Benefit Analysis**: Reviews the pricing structure, total cost of ownership, and the overall value provided by the technology partner.
- **Financial Impact**: Ensures that investment aligns with the budget constraints and financial goals while assessing the return on investment and long-term financial benefits.
- **Budget Approval**: May need to approve expenditures and financial commitments related to the technology partnership.

Chief Technology Officer (CTO)

- **Technology Leadership**: Provides insights into the technical viability of the partner's solutions, including their compatibility with current and future technology needs.
- **Innovation and Scalability**: Evaluates how well the partner's technology aligns with the organization's technology roadmap and ability to scale.
- **Integration**: Assesses the feasibility of integrating the partner's solutions with existing systems and infrastructure.

Business Unit Head (BU Head)

- **Operational Impact**: Evaluate how the technology partner's solutions will address specific needs and challenges within their business unit.
- **Performance and ROI**: Assesses the potential impact on operational efficiency, productivity, and achievement of business unit objectives.
- **User Needs**: Provides input on how well the technology meets the unique requirements and goals of the specific business unit.

Head of Procurement or Sourcing

- **Vendor Selection**: Manages the procurement process, including issuing RFPs, negotiating terms, and evaluating vendor proposals.
- **Contract Management**: Oversees the contractual aspects of the partnership, ensuring that terms align with organizational requirements and policies.
- **Cost Efficiency**: Evaluates pricing structures and ensures cost-effectiveness while securing favorable terms for the organization.

External Consultants or Advisors

- **Expert Evaluation:** Provide independent assessments of the technology partner's capabilities and their alignment with organizational needs.
- **Best Practices**: Offer insights based on industry experience and best practices, guiding the selection process.
- **Strategic Advice**: Advice on the overall strategic alignment and potential impact of the technology partnership on the organization's goals.

Project Management Office (PMO)

- **Project Alignment**: Ensures the technology partner's solutions align with overall project goals and strategic initiatives.
- **Governance and Oversight**: Monitors adherence to project management standards, timelines, and budget. Evaluates the partner's ability to manage and execute the project effectively.
- **Risk Management**: Assesses potential risks associated with the technology partner and their solutions, ensuring that risks are identified and mitigated throughout the project lifecycle.

Security, Risk, and Compliance Officer

- **Security and Risk Management**: Evaluate the partner's security measures, including data protection and risk mitigation strategies.
- **Regulatory and Policy Compliance**: Ensures the solutions adhere to relevant regulations, industry standards, and internal policies.
- **Audit and Reporting**: Monitors compliance documentation and reporting to ensure transparency and adherence to legal requirements.

The Role of Delegates in Representing End Users' Interests

These team leaders, appointed by their BU heads, provide daily support to partner teams in areas such as process understanding, data analysis, user interviews, and user acceptance testing. Their close collaboration with the partner team allows them to wield significant influence during the evaluation process.

- **Functional Needs**: Provides input on how the technology partner's solutions meet the specific needs and requirements of their team or department.

- **Usability and Efficiency**: Assesses the technology's ease of use and its impact on team productivity and efficiency, providing feedback on practical aspects and any issues encountered.
- **Adoption and Training**: Evaluate the support and training provided by the partner to ensure smooth adoption and effective use of the technology by end users.

While some decision-makers are highly involved during the partner evaluation process, they tend to disengage after a decision has been made, except for key figures like the CDO, CIO, CTO, and the sponsoring BU Head. However, a lack of alignment on priorities among these stakeholders, such as the CIO, CDO, or BU Head, can sometimes cause friction.

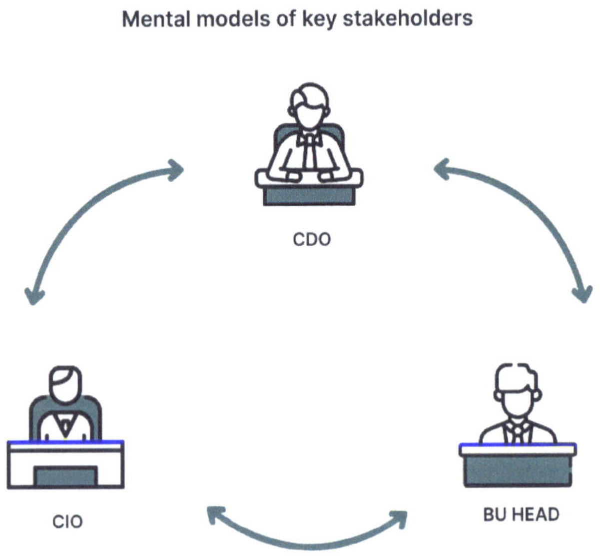

Diagram 14: Key Stakeholders of Digital Transformation

"Have you faced challenges in aligning these stakeholders?"

Where is the lack of alignment arising from?

The differing priorities of the CIO, CDO, and BU Head significantly impact project execution. The CIO focuses on the stability and scalability of IT infrastructure, the CDO prioritizes digital innovation and user experience, and the BU Head is concerned with achieving business outcomes and revenue targets.

But do they recognize the common interests that unite their efforts? Why is it so challenging for them to align?

"What we often perceive are only surface-level issues. The true source of misalignment often lies deeper, rooted in the unique perspectives shaped by each stakeholder's individual experiences."

Caselet 2

"During the first week of a digital transformation program kick-off for a mid-sized bank in India, we hit a significant roadblock. The Head of Business and the Head of IT were at odds. I was representing the partner's team, responsible for helping them build digital journeys to enable their D2C customers to open CASA accounts online. The Head of Business had already committed to a launch date, while the Head of IT wasn't even sure if the necessary ecosystem APIs were available in the production environment to support this capability.

Fifteen minutes into the conversation, I recognized the political sensitivity and the firm stances of both stakeholders. I suggested we adjourn the meeting and arrange one-on-one discussions with each of them.

After some probing, I discovered that the Head of Business had already communicated the launch date to external stakeholders, including the media. We discussed a workaround: using the UAT version of the APIs to stage the savings account journey for the media, allowing the launch to proceed as planned.

With this solution in hand, I approached the Head of IT, who readily agreed. Aligning stakeholders with different yet valid perspectives often requires finding common ground and viewing the situation through a neutral lens to appreciate both points of view."

4.2 Unique Mental Models

Our actions and behaviors reflect our distinct mental models, which are influenced by our personal experiences and lead to varied perspectives. Understanding these underlying differences is crucial for effective collaboration.

CIO Mental Model: Stability and Scalability

- **Career path:** Often starts as *a* system analyst or in similar technical roles, rising through the ranks to IT management and leadership positions.
- **Focus**: Ensuring the reliability, security, and efficiency of the IT infrastructure.
- **Key concerns:** Defect density, code coverage, RCA (Root Cause Analysis) of critical defects, and alignment with enterprise architecture.
- **Approach:** Emphasizes risk management, process optimization, and long-term technological sustainability.
- **View on technology**: Views technology as the backbone of the organization, essential for supporting business operations and ensuring continuity.

CDO Mental Model: Innovation and User Experience

- **Career path:** Often starts in roles related to digital marketing, product management, or IT innovation, rising through the ranks with a focus on digital transformation initiatives.

- **Focus**: Driving digital transformation, enhancing user experience, and leveraging new technologies.
- **Key concerns:** Digital innovation, speed to market, user engagement metrics, and adoption of cutting-edge technologies.
- **Approach**: Favors agile methodologies, rapid prototyping, and continuous improvement to stay ahead of market trends and customer expectations.
- **View on technology**: Sees technology as a means to innovate, improve user experiences, and drive competitive advantage.

BU Head Mental Model: Business Outcomes and Revenue

- **Career path**: Often starts in sales, marketing, or operations, rising through the ranks to manage business units with a strong focus on financial performance and strategic initiatives.
- **Focus:** Achieving business objectives, maximizing revenue, and improving operational efficiency.
- **Key concerns**: Revenue uplift, cost savings, user experience, cross-sell/upsell opportunities, and business impact of IT solutions.
- **Approach:** Prioritizes projects and initiatives that directly contribute to business goals, often pushing for quick results and measurable outcomes.
- **View on technology**: Sees technology as a tool to drive business growth, enhance efficiency, and achieve strategic objectives.

Visualize this: Three individuals in the early stages of their careers, each immersed in their specialized field:

- **Person A** is deeply engaged in resolving critical defects and performing root cause analysis in production systems, focused on troubleshooting and system stability.

- **Person B** is dedicated to analyzing digital marketing funnels and user behavior, specializing in optimizing customer journeys and digital engagement strategies.
- **Person C** is concentrated on meeting sales targets and managing team incentives, driven by goals related to revenue generation and motivational strategies.

"Their distinct roles and experiences naturally lead them to have different perspectives, shaped by their unique areas of expertise and daily challenges."

As these three individuals grow into roles as CIO, CDO, and BU Head, their distinct experiences will profoundly influence their perspectives:

- **The CIO** will have a focus on system stability and technology infrastructure, driven by their background in resolving critical defects and ensuring operational reliability.
- **The CDO** will prioritize digital innovation and user experience, shaped by their expertise in digital marketing and user behavior analytics.
- **The BU Head** will concentrate on achieving business outcomes and revenue targets, influenced by their experience in managing sales performance and team incentives

"Don't you think that conflict between these individuals is due to their unique mental models?"

Yes, each person's experiences and expertise shape their priorities and viewpoints, leading to differing approaches and objectives.

Recognizing these differences and addressing them through open communication and collaborative problem-solving is crucial for aligning their efforts and achieving shared objectives.

It's natural for stakeholders from Tech, Digital, Marketing, and Business to bring varying perspectives to the table. Progress occurs when these individuals collaborate to find common ground on which solutions can be developed.

Here are a few key strategies that may foster better collaboration:

- **Aligning on Common Interests**: Identifying common interests, developing a shared understanding, and aligning them on their interests can benefit the entire organization. Rather than focusing on all the metrics, teams should align on minimal viable success metrics.
- **Integrating Perspectives:** Develop strategies that address the needs and goals of each role, ensuring that technology, digital initiatives, and business objectives are aligned.
- **Effective Communication:** A leader must embrace and encourage open and transparent communication between their teams. Using common vocabulary and avoiding technical jargon are key steps toward fostering mutual understanding and respect.
- **Cross-Functional Teams:** It's often found that these teams work in silos. Leaders must ensure the creation of cross-functional teams that include members from each team to encourage collaboration and knowledge sharing to foster innovation.
- **Flexible Methodologies**: Each team can not operate at different ends of the methodologies. It's often seen digital and business teams prefer agility and IT teams are linear and sequential in their approach. Each team should strive to come to a common point and create hybrid methodologies that provide collaboration, flexibility, and some level of iterative development. Involving key members from each team (IT, Digital, and Business) in the

planning and execution of projects is one good way to ensure finding common ground and collective buy-in.

Can AI play a crucial role in decision making?

"AI is unlikely to fully replace human decision-making roles but will instead enhance their capabilities, at least in the near future."

Key executives will continue to play an important role in addressing the potential lack of alignments among stakeholders by fostering collaboration, ensuring transparency, and integrating diverse perspectives. Given AI's limitations, such as over-reliance on historical data and the risk of bias, interpreting AI-generated patterns will ultimately depend on human judgment, critical thinking, and collaboration.

4.3 Done is better than Perfect Vs First Time Right

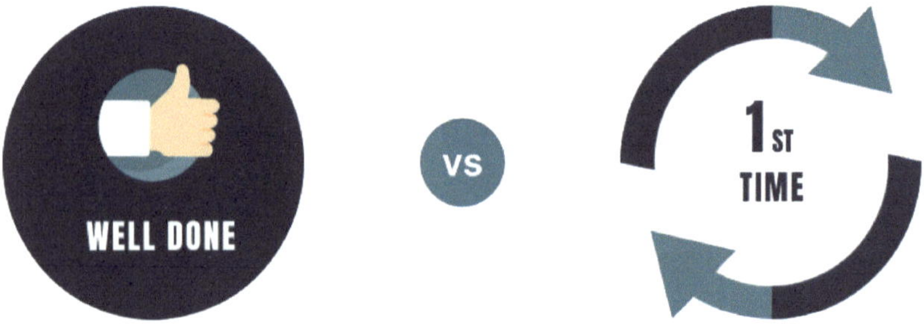

Diagram 15: Done is better than perfect vs First Time Right

Caselet 3

"I vividly remember the night we were preparing to deploy our newly built website to production. I had to work closely with both the Head of IT and the Head of E-Commerce, coordinating efforts with our implementation partner. The website included a new buying engine, and tensions were high. The Head of IT was adamant about ensuring the build was of the highest quality, with no critical defects

left unresolved. On the other hand, the Head of E-Commerce was focused on preserving our SEO legacy, insisting that every link from the old site be migrated to maintain affiliate and directory links, which were essential for our SEO strategy moving forward. The team felt the strain of being pulled in different directions until the Head of Digital stepped in as a mediator.

*His goal was to get the new website launched, gather customer feedback on the new features, and then iterate for future releases. In every meeting, he would emphasize the mantra, "**Done is better than perfect.**"*

This phrase resonated with me and prompted me to reflect more deeply on these two distinct approaches.

In the context of "Done is better than perfect," 'Done' doesn't mean 100% completion. It's more like the term 'OK' in some colloquial contexts - an acceptance that something is good enough to move forward. It implies that you've made sufficient progress to avoid getting bogged down by perfectionism. On the other hand, some individuals strive for 'First Time Right,' prioritizing getting everything correct from the outset.

These two distinct mindsets lead to different approaches in how projects are conceived and executed. Let's delve into these approaches further.

Progress over Perfection

1. **Mindset**:
    - Emphasizes speed and momentum over high quality at the outset.
    - Encourages starting early or completing a task quickly, even if it's not flawless.

- Focuses on getting feedback early and iterating based on that feedback.

2. **Approach**:

   - Often used with agile methodologies where iterative development and continuous improvement are prioritized.
   - Promotes the idea that delivering something functional quickly can be more valuable than waiting to deliver a perfect product.
   - Encourages taking risks, experimenting, and learning from mistakes.

3. **Benefits**:

   - Faster time to market.
   - Quicker feedback loops from users or stakeholders.
   - Flexibility to adapt and make changes based on real-world use and feedback.

4. **Challenges**:

   - This may result in lower initial quality or incomplete features.
   - Potential for technical debt if quick fixes are not addressed later.
   - This can lead to a perception of lower standards if not managed properly.

First Time Right (FTR)

1. **Mindset**

   - Emphasizes accuracy in completing tasks correctly the first time.
   - Aims to minimize errors and defects from the outset to avoid rework and additional costs.
   - Focuses on thorough planning, quality control, and meticulous execution.

2. **Approach**:
    - It is often used in project scenarios where mistakes can be costly.
    - Involves extensive upfront analysis, detailed documentation, and rigorous testing before delivering the final product.
    - Encourages a mindset of excellence and high standards from the beginning.
3. **Benefits**:
    - Higher initial quality and fewer defects.
    - Reduced rework and associated costs.
    - Enhanced reliability and customer satisfaction.
4. **Challenges**:
    - Longer development cycles and delayed time to market.
    - Potential for over-engineering and excessive documentation.
    - Less flexibility to adapt to changes or feedback once the project is underway.

What do these approaches focus on?

Speed vs. Quality:

"Progress over perfection" prioritizes speed and getting something functional out quickly, while "First Time Right" prioritizes quality and accuracy from the outset.

Iterative vs. Linear:

"Progress over perfection"aligns with iterative development and continuous improvement, whereas "First Time Right" aligns with a more linear and thorough approach to ensure correctness.

Risk Management:

"Progress over perfection" is more accepting of initial risks and mistakes, leveraging them as learning opportunities, whereas "First Time Right" seeks to minimize risks and mistakes through careful planning and execution.

Flexibility:

"Progress over perfection" allows for greater flexibility and adaptability, while "First Time Right" requires a more rigid adherence to plans and standards.

While both approaches have their merits and can be chosen based on the context, project goals, and organizational culture. The key is to understand the trade-offs and select the approach that best aligns with the specific needs and priorities of the project or organization.

And how are these approaches linked to key decision makers?

First Time Right (FTR). This approach helps with minimizing disruptions. I have seen CIO's performance linked to system stability and low tech debt in production systems, that pushes them to emphasize thorough planning and high quality delivery each time a build hits the production environment. You will find many CIOs leaning towards the FTR approach and may be averse to taking risks and jeopardize the system stability where customers are interacting with your solutions.

There are a few CIO's who are forward looking and are willing to experiment with new ideas, innovative technology and test their solution in a controlled user group (CUG) environment. However, their DNA may prohibit them from putting a not-fully-tested solution in the PROD and taking the risks of business downtown.

Progress over Perfection. This approach favors agility and rapid iteration. A typical CDO persona will prefer this approach because it allows for quick experimentation of new digital solutions. This enables them to rapidly gather user feedback and iterate, which is crucial in fast-paced digital environments where innovation and speed are key to staying competitive. They aim to revolutionize business processes and customer experiences, viewing digital transformation as a critical path to maintaining a competitive edge. This urgency often leads them to favor riskier, yet potentially more rewarding, approaches.

The differing priorities and approaches can lead to disagreements between CDOs and CIOs. I have seen many CDOs viewing CIOs as overly cautious and resistant to change, while CIOs perceive CDOs as too aggressive and willing to compromise stability for the sake of innovation.

Balanced Approach: There is a need to bring a balance between speed and quality. It requires a careful consideration of project goals, the organization's appetite to take calculated risks, and risk management strategies. If an initiative requires rapid market entry or testing an idea and iterating the solution based on customer feedback, it might need a leaning towards "Progress over perfection" approach. However, for critical projects that directly impact the business's core operations and profitability, it could be a strong use case for leaning towards "First Time Right". I have seen Business Heads bringing this perspective to the table and lead the discussion towards choosing the approach based on their project's goals and risks.

Sometimes, the PMO head effectively facilitates risk identification and mitigation discussions, ensuring that the CIO, CDO, and Business Heads are well-informed and can make the right decisions.

Additionally, rapid prototyping enabled by AI tools and technologies may help in validating certain hypotheses quickly to help with more informed decision making.

Chapter 5

Exploring Commercial Models in Digital Transformation

5.0 What are the commercial models clients are looking for?

Having understood the various stakeholders, decision-makers and influencers as part of client organizations who are responsible for evaluating the right technology partners to help them choose and implement the most relevant technology solution for their business growth, it becomes equally important for us to understand the commercial models available that help establish partnership between clients and technology partners.

5.1 Common commercial models

While there could be many variants of commercial models that the technology industry may be using, broadly all of them can be bucketed in one of these models. We will have a brief look at each one of them and understand why they are preferred. We will double click on some of them to understand the complexity behind those models.

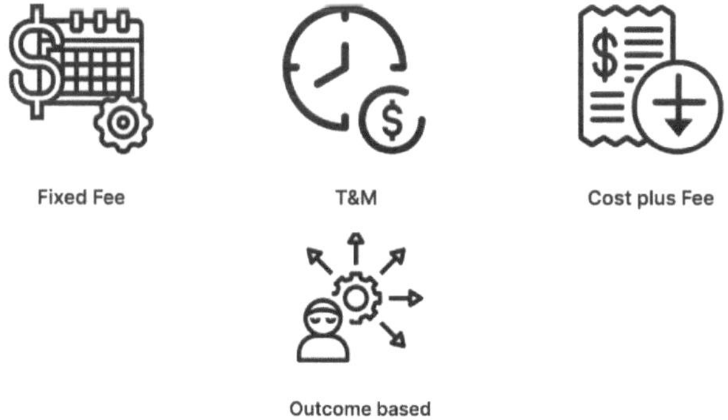

Diagram 16: Common Commercial Models

5.1.1 T&M (Time and Materials) Model

How does this work?

In this commercial arrangement, client and partners agree on a tiered or blended rate card for the combination of skills, grades, seniority, and geography of the team offered by the partner. Partners would bill them for the amount of hours clocked by their team on a weekly or on monthly basis after applying the agreed rate. Both parties may agree to 'Max Cap' for weekly hours or a monthly budget.

When would clients prefer this?

There could be a **couple of scenarios** why clients may prefer this option.

When client stakeholders understand the scope of work very well and see little to no risks in the execution. They may have the core skills, capability, and willingness to control the execution of the project. They believe that they can get the execution done at a relatively lesser cost by adding a few consultants or contractors to their existing team for the complementary skill sets they need.

At times, clients are in the R&D or innovation stage of their product development and want to develop a few hypotheses to test. They may need a few experts from a specific niche skill set or domain but don't want to give away the entire control of their IPR (Intellectual Property Rights). They may be running behind the timeline, may not have enough time to hire a Full Time Employee, and therefore, want to quickly onboard contractors or consultants until their product strategy is firmed up. This engagement model can also be seen as a staff augmentation or co-source model.

When would Partners prefer this?

For partners, this contract model is the least risky. The client's project manager takes charge of planning and assigning work, while the partner team is expected to deliver quality work and track their hours each week. The client's supervisor reviews the team's progress and provides feedback as needed.

However, in practice, clients may still expect the partner team to complete certain tasks within a pre-agreed timeframe, leading to the usual project management challenges around scope, timing, and risks. In such cases, the partner's project manager may need to manage these aspects, even though billing follows the T&M model.

What's in it for the Team?

In this type of engagement, especially with maintenance or support work, team morale can be a challenge. The work might not be as exciting for the partner's team, especially if it lacks opportunities for transformation or innovation. This can lead to lower motivation and possibly higher attrition rates.

5.1.2 Fixed Bid Model

How does this work?

In a Fixed Bid arrangement, the client agrees to pay a fixed fee for the partner's services. The scope is outlined at a high to mid-level, with tentative agreements on timelines and quality expectations. Payments are tied to delivery milestones and often include clauses for risks and rewards, covering any delays or issues that could impact payments. Clients typically issue an RFP or share project details with a few selected partners, evaluating their responses based on criterias such as quality, capability, and cost.

When would clients prefer this?

Clients might prefer this approach when they have a clear vision of the product but aren't confident in managing the software development process and want to minimize execution risks. If the project is complex, involving multiple vendors or ecosystem integration, and the budget is fixed by top management, clients often choose the RFP route and favor a Fixed Bid option.

When would Partners prefer this?

In a competitive environment where multiple service providers are bidding, the focus often shifts to outbidding others. The success of these engagements depends heavily on the expertise of those shaping the proposals. Partner teams bring in domain experts, program managers, and technologists to set clear boundaries around scope, design, and dependencies to protect against expected risks, while also adding buffers for unforeseen challenges.

However, this setup can be risky for partners, as they might have to cover cost overruns due to delays or scope creep. Consequently, service providers often take on these risks in hopes of securing long-term partnerships.

What's in it for the Team?

The team needs to stay alert for scope-creep and regularly negotiate changes that require client approval and payment. Agreed-upon changes usually affect effort, timeline, and cost, requiring constant realignment. Managing these change requests is essential but can be challenging, often adding pressure that may lead to stress, low motivation, and even attrition.

Leaders of Fixed Bid programs should be aware of this and protect their teams from unnecessary pressure due to uncertainties in scope and timeline. They are expected to navigate the program successfully by carefully balancing the trade-offs.

5.1.3 Cost plus fee contract

How does it work?

This contracting model is often used to set up large offshore development teams for clients. It includes direct costs like employee salaries, along with an agreed-upon management fee. Clients maintain full control over the work and management of the staff at these centers, while partners take care of administrative tasks such as leasing space, providing security, recruiting staff, setting up development processes, and overseeing the team's growth and capabilities.

When would clients prefer this?

When clients want to expand operations internationally and build technology capabilities in low-cost countries, they may choose this option. By focusing on their core strengths and offshoring non-core functions like technology and business operations to cost-effective service providers, clients can balance business risks and gain the advantage of a business continuity plan (BCP) in case of disaster recovery in a multi-geo business environment.

When would partners prefer this?

Partners might prefer the cost-plus-fee model because it provides flexibility and ensures comprehensive coverage of all project-related expenses, including salaries and administrative costs. By using this model, partners can manage the complexities of setting up and running large offshore development teams while being assured of compensation for actual costs incurred plus a management fee.

What's in it for the Team?

This model often ensures that the team has the necessary resources and support, as partners are incentivized to cover all relevant costs and invest in quality infrastructure and development processes. This model can lead to better working conditions and access to training and growth opportunities, as partners are motivated to maintain high standards to meet client expectations. Additionally, with clients retaining control over work and management, the project team benefits from clear direction and expectations, aligning their efforts more effectively with project goals.

Differences in working methods and cultural nuances between client and partner teams can occasionally lead to contention. However, with effort, it's possible to develop a common approach that accommodates both sides and fosters effective collaboration.

5.1.4 Outcome-based model

How does it work?

This model is a variation of the Fixed Bid approach, with the key difference being that a portion of the agreed-upon fee is variable and tied to specific outcomes, based on mutually agreed-upon metrics between the client and the partner. For this model to be effective, there must be strong alignment between client stakeholders and the partner leadership team, ensuring openness and transparency in communication, data exchange, and the methods used to baseline and periodically measure these metrics.

When would clients prefer this?

Clients may opt for this model when they want the partners to have a vested interest in the project's success. Whether it is for testing a new product feature in the market or adding a new revenue channel, this approach allows for some level of experimentation, with risks and rewards shared between the client and the partner. This setup can help safeguard the client's investment, especially when penalty clauses are included in the contract to mitigate potential losses.

When would partners prefer this?

A partner would prefer an outcome-based model when they have confidence in their ability to deliver strong results and see the potential for a high return on investment. This model is appealing to partners who excel in innovation and are eager to demonstrate their expertise in driving impactful outcomes. It's also a preferred option when the partner wants to build a long-term relationship with the client, as it aligns their incentives with the client's success. Additionally, partners may choose this model if they have experience in similar projects and are confident in managing risks, knowing that their performance will directly influence their financial rewards.

What's in it for the Team?

For the project team, an outcome-based model offers several benefits. Firstly, it can foster a sense of ownership and motivation, as the team's efforts are directly tied to the project's success and the potential rewards. This model often encourages greater collaboration, innovation, and problem-solving, as the team is incentivized to find the most effective solutions to meet or exceed the desired outcomes.

Additionally, working under an outcome-based model can provide the project team with a clear focus on results rather than just tasks, leading to a greater sense of purpose and accomplishment. The potential for recognition and financial rewards tied to performance can also boost morale and drive the team to deliver their best work.

Lastly, success in such a model can enhance the team's reputation and credibility, leading to more opportunities for challenging and rewarding projects in the future. This creates a win-win situation for the client, the partner, and the project team.

Fixed Fee	T&M	Cost plus Fee	Outcome based
Understand problem, scope behind the proposed solution and estimate the effort needed and response with a fixed quote along with assumptions (guard rails)	Understand the problem and suggest a team with right skill sets and their price points (rate cards)	Understand the problem, suggest a team, skill sets and their cost structure along with other administrative effort to translate as professional fee	Understand problem, desired outcomes, solution paths to reach to those outcomes, key metrics and their measurement methods and propose a commercial model
More risks for vendors	Less risks for vendors	Least risky for vendors	High risks, high gains
Needs strong program management skills	Desired low to medium program management	Needs low to medium program management skills	Needs strong domain, consulting and program management skills
Needs strong CR management skills to address Change Requests	Needs less CR management skills to address changes	Needs Less CR management skills to address changes	Less moderate CR skills as value driven prioritization helps
Vendor pm in control	Client PM in control	Client PM in control	Both PMs are co-driving
Core team (BA, PM, TL) rotation is not preferred in short-mid term	Team rotation is norm	Team rotation is always with a approval	Key team members rotation may impact engagement outcomes

Diagram 17: Common Commercial Models - A Comparison View

5.2 The Variants of Fixed-Bid Models

Fixed Bid Commercial models have come in various forms. While these variants may have implications on the commercial structure at the time of signing the agreement, they must be understood from an execution perspective. I will address both aspects of Fixed Bids from the perspectives of contracting and successful delivery.

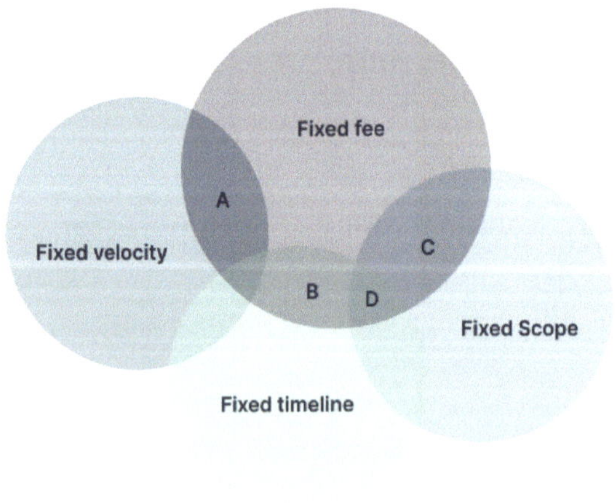

Diagram 18: The Variants of Fixed Bid Models

A. Fixed Capacity (aka Fixed Fee and Fixed Velocity)

How does this work?

In this commercial arrangement, two parties agree on a pre-committed delivery velocity for a fixed fee, without a defined scope. Delivery velocity is measured in Story Points or another agreed-upon unit. The client retains ownership of the product backlog, developing and assigning stories based on the team's anticipated velocity. The partner's team bills the client a monthly rate for the agreed capacity. If there are any spikes or changes in scope, the partner's team is notified in advance to adjust capacity as needed, and a change order is processed to account for the commercial impact.

When would clients prefer this?

Clients may prefer this model for transformation programs when they've already defined the product vision and roadmap, with most of their backlog prepared, although some items still require analysis and design. In such cases, they might select a partner with the right skills for staff augmentation at a fixed fee. This approach is similar to Time and Materials (T&M) but includes a commitment from the partner's team to maintain consistent delivery speed. It helps clients manage their budget effectively, ensuring costs stay within the set amount for additional work.

When would partners prefer this?

For partners, this model presents a lower-risk alternative to Fixed Bid because the client prioritizes scope each sprint, minimizing or eliminating the risk of scope creep. The partner deploys a fixed capacity based on the client's requirements for team configuration and maintains some reserve capacity to handle leaves, unplanned vacations, or emergencies. After a few months of collaboration and a deeper understanding of the tasks, partners can more accurately plan and refine their commitment to a delivery velocity that suits both parties.

What's in it for the team?

In a lower-pressure program scenario, the team generally finds it easier to navigate. However, without a shared vocabulary and clear definitions for work units (such as Story Points) and their calculation, meeting fixed velocity commitments can be challenging initially. Developing a mutual understanding of work units, based on the nature of the tasks and the technology landscape, is crucial for the team's success.

Additionally, if the staff augmentation is for routine maintenance and support, keeping the team motivated becomes another challenge. Teams can quickly fall into a monotonous routine, so the partner needs to implement a rotation plan to maintain engagement and motivation.

B. Fixed Fee and Fixed Time

How does this work?

In a Fixed Fee and Fixed Time arrangement, the partner commits to delivering the agreed-upon program objectives or scope within a predetermined time frame for a fixed sum. Both the fee and the timeline are established at the beginning based on a high to mid-level understanding of the program's requirements. The service provider invoices the client upon reaching pre-agreed milestones, ensuring that payments align with the project's progress. This model requires careful planning and clear agreement on deliverables to mitigate risks and manage expectations effectively.

When would clients prefer this?

When the clients lack clarity on the target state and have a low-risk tolerance, they invite potential service providers to bid on the program. The contract is typically awarded to the partner with the relevant skills who is willing to accept some execution risks. The business team may prioritize factors like product launches or marketing campaigns, which can influence the timeline. Their focus is primarily on achieving predefined outcomes rather than the program's detailed scope, meanwhile, the IT team must adhere to a fixed budget allocated during their annual budget planning, which dictates their financial constraints for the program.

When would partners prefer this?

Partners with a deep understanding of the business domain are often preferred, as they are willing to take on the risks associated with limiting the scope to meet program objectives and deliver within the agreed-upon timeline. Their expertise allows them to navigate uncertainties and manage the project effectively within defined constraints. Additionally, partners may sometimes offer aggressive bids to secure new business, even outbidding incumbent partners, to establish a foothold with new clients and showcase their capabilities. While this competitive approach can lead to significant cost advantages for clients, it also requires careful evaluation of the provider's ability to meet the program's needs.

What's in it for the team?

Although the fees and timelines are fixed, teams can use their reprioritization skills to manage the scope within the program objectives. They may influence clients to view scope changes as **legitimate Change Requests**, using their domain expertise to secure additional payments. Effective program management is essential for addressing missed dependencies and adapting to shifting timelines. Since the partner's team usually controls these aspects, achieving the desired outcomes is often within reach.

C. Fixed Fee and Fixed Scope

How does this work?

In this commercial arrangement, the partner agrees to deliver the mutually defined program scope for a fixed amount of money. Both the program fee and scope are negotiated upfront, based on a shared understanding of the project details. To facilitate this process, clients typically issue a Request for Proposal (RFP) and provide common Q&A forums to address partners' queries before bids are submitted.

When would clients prefer this?

Clients might prefer a Fixed Fee and Fixed Scope arrangement when they have a clear understanding of the project's scope but are uncertain about 'how' to achieve it In such cases, they aim to transfer the execution risks to the partners, who are responsible for determining and implementing the most effective technical approach to solve the problem. Clients expect partners to leverage their expertise to propose solutions and deliver the agreed-upon scope for a fixed sum of money. This model is beneficial for clients who want to manage their budgets effectively while relying on partners to handle the complexities and risks of execution.

Why would partners prefer this?

Partners may prefer this model during the bidding process to differentiate themselves from competitors. To gain an advantage, some service providers bring in subject matter experts (SMEs) to clearly define scope boundaries and establish guardrails, enabling them to effectively manage the program's scope, risks, and dependencies. Additionally, partners might see potential benefits from various change requests that arise during the project. This model also provides an opportunity to build long-term relationships with clients by demonstrating their capability to deliver within fixed parameters while managing evolving needs.

What's in it for the team?

This type of program demands a highly proactive team and strict program management to succeed. While the intensity of such programs can lead to burnout, having a program coach and mentors is essential for providing guidance and clarity throughout the process. Despite its demanding nature, the program offers significant opportunities for growth and learning, as long as there is strong governance and proactive management. This challenging environment serves as an excellent platform for team members to develop their skills and advance their careers.

D. Fixed Fee, Fixed Scope, and Fixed Time

How does it work?

In this model, the partner team commits to delivering the defined program scope for a fixed amount of money within a predetermined timeline. This arrangement is typically used for high-priority RFPs and involves senior executives to ensure clarity and alignment throughout the bidding process. Additionally, executives from both the client and service provider are actively involved in overseeing the program, managing escalations, and ensuring that the project stays on track.

Why would clients prefer this?

In this scenario, the client generally has a clear understanding of the project scope but may be uncertain regarding the technical approach. They may also face numerous internal and external dependencies that are challenging to manage alone. As a result, they prefer to outsource the project to a partner who can handle the complete execution and associated third-party risks. This approach allows the client to leverage the expertise of external vendors to navigate complex dependencies and execute the project efficiently, while transferring the risks involved.

Why would partners prefer this?

Partners might prefer this model because it provides an opportunity to establish long-term partnerships with clients. To differentiate themselves from competitors, they may bring in domain experts and leverage program accelerators to enhance their proposal. Successfully managing such engagements can lead to significant benefits, including the potential for future projects and ongoing business relationships. By demonstrating their ability to handle complex projects effectively, partners can build a strong reputation and secure more opportunities for growth and collaboration.

	Fixed Capacity (A)	Fixed Fee and Fixed Time (B)	Fixed Fee and Fixed Scope (C)	Fixed Fee, Fixed Scope & Fixed Time (D)
How does it work	Precommitted delivery velocity for Fixed Fee. Execution is similar to T&M. Monthly billing	Expected to deliver agreed program objectives within predetermined time and Fixed Fee. Billing as per delivery milestone	Expected to deliver agreed program scope within negotiated Fixed Fee, usually via RFP. Billing as per delivery milestone	Expected to deliver the mutually agreed program scope for a fixed sum of money within a pre-set timeline. High priority RFPs. Billing as per delivery milestone
Why Clients prefer	Product roadmap, backlog is available. Need to augment the team to accelerate delivery	Less clarity in target state, poor risk appetite. Launch dates are more important than features	May have a good clarity of target state but don't know how to get there	May Have a good clarity of project scope but can't manage internal and external dependencies
Why Partners prefer	Less revenue risk for Service providers, no scope creep conversations	Would like to mitigate the risk by applying domain skills to pull through the agreed program objectives	Outcompete others in RFPs, Bring SMEs & PM Expertise to create scope guard rails. Long term relationships.	May leverage accelerators and domain experts to create faster value. Long term relationships.
Achievability	Always achievable	Mostly achievable	Aggressive but possible	Almost impossible

Diagram 19: The Variants of Fixed Bid Models - A Comparison View

What's in it for the team?

This type of engagement demands strong expertise in domain knowledge, program management, and risk governance from both sides to succeed. The high-pressure environment makes it challenging to balance constraints like scope, time, and budget, while maintaining quality, making it difficult to achieve win-win outcomes. However, team members in such programs face a steep learning curve in domain and program management skills, making the experience challenging but rewarding if managed effectively.

Additionally, continuous negotiation over scope and timelines with key client stakeholders is necessary throughout the program lifecycle, which can lead to fatigue. This requires ongoing attention from senior leadership to ensure the team stays motivated and focused.

5.3 Outcome-based Commercial Models

Among the various commercial models in the technology industry, the outcome-based commercial models are the most complex and riskiest. As they say, "high risks, high gains," this model may offer a huge promise of upside, if played well.

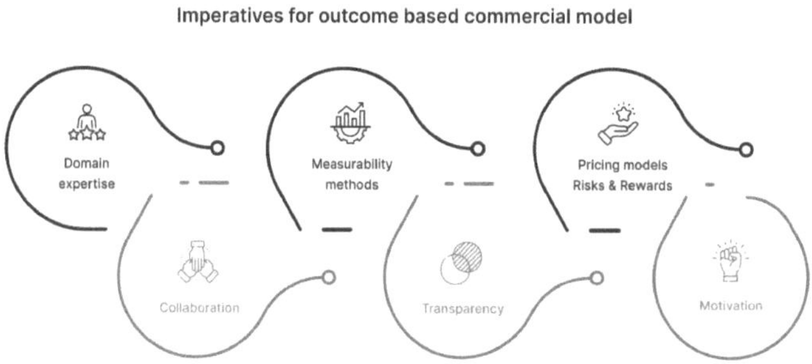

Diagram 20: The Principles of Outcome-based Commercial Models

So, how does this work? And why would clients opt for such a model?

Let me illustrate this with an example of home renovation.

Imagine you're renovating your kitchen, bathrooms, bedrooms, and living area. You have a budget and need a good team for the job. You might consider three options to find the best fit for your project:

1. Hire a team of specialist on daily wages (T&M)
2. Hire a contractor for a Fixed Quote
3. Hire a contractor for Successful Outcomes with linkage to rewards and penalties

Option 1: Hire a team of specialists on daily wages.

You are almost entirely invested in the model, taking all smaller or bigger decisions of execution, procuring all the materials by yourself and making them available as per the project sequence. You may need a small storage area to manage the minimum inventory to prevent any work from being hampered due to the shortage of materials. You have to supervise all the activities to ensure productivity and quality of work. Daily wage workers who are working for you may not be motivated for the job all the time. They understand that they will get paid their daily wages for the number of hours on the job, regardless of the speed or quality of their work. Of course, you can fire them for not doing a good job, but you are also carrying a risk of the job getting delayed each time there is a hand-off. Additionally, your team may lose enthusiasm after a few weeks if left unmonitored, so you must remain vigilant and actively engaged throughout the process.

Net-net, as a client, you are playing all roles – project sponsor, project manager, supervisor, procurement, etc. if you are getting the job done on a Time and Materials (T&M) basis.

Option 2: Hire a contractor for a Fixed Quote

In this scenario, you explain the work (scope, quality expectations, specification for the makeover, timeline expectations, etc.) to a contractor and expect a fixed quote. There are two possibilities for a fixed quote:

One is with a fixed labor quote where you are responsible for procuring all the materials, and the other is where you outsource everything for a fixed price that includes both materials and labor. You can expect multiple contractors to share their quotes.

After conducting due diligence, you choose one contractor and proceed. The contractor may provide their Statement of Work (SOW) at the outset, which typically includes scope, specifications of materials and payment terms tied to delivery milestones amongst many other details. The contractor's team manages and supervises the entire project, but you may need to engage at certain levels to ensure that the quality of work meets your expectations. Contractors may try to cut corners on certain aspects that are not immediately visible to complete their milestones for timely payments. Some contractors might work faster to achieve their payment milestones, potentially compromising quality that you would notice only after moving in. Some clients may withhold a portion of the amount for the warranty period.

Option 3: Hire a contractor for Successful Outcomes with Risks and Rewards

In this case, you explain your work (scope, quality expectations, specification of makeover, timeline expectations, etc.) to a few contractors and outline the successful outcome of your project. During the evaluation stage, you propose breaking the Quoted price into two parts: one fixed and the other variable. Craft your variable in such a way that, upon the successful achievement of the expected outcome, the contractors receive more than the contracted variable amount. And in case of underachievement, they get penalized.

This model may motivate your contractor to do a good job and deliver your work within agreed-upon timelines and uncompromised quality. An example of a reward could be 20% and 15% extra payment on the SOW variable amount if the project is completed two months ahead of time with NO compromise on quality. Similarly, an example of a penalty could be a 20% or 30% penalty on the SOW variable amount if the project is delayed by 2 or 3 months respectively. An additional 15% penalty could be applied if the quality of work is not as per your expectations.

The most critical aspect of this model is establishing a common understanding of quality and timelines, along with how to measure them consistently over time.

The third option seems rewarding for contractors, but it requires a greater risk appetite. For you, the client, it takes away most of your headache of supervising people and constantly keeping them motivated, though it comes at a relatively higher price.

"How does this model work in the technology world, where the outcomes are not as tangible as in a home renovation with matching specs of tiling, furnishing, etc?"

First and foremost, while you might skip a formal agreement for a small home renovation, in a structured industry like technology, commercial agreements require thorough legal review to ensure the enforcement of risks and reward clauses.

A few key factors behind this modeling in the technology Industry are:

- As a client, you have an onus of explaining what a good outcome looks like and how to measure it transparently. Open communication throughout the program's lifecycle goes a long way in building trust between two parties and paves the foundation for this model to work.
- As a partner, you are expected to show your skin in the game. You are taking a bet on the achievement of the client's objectives. That would mean, you are expected to understand their business and associated variables that play up in their outcome creation.

Let's explore some of the typical metrics that clients and partners might use when building outcome-based commercial models in the technology space. Below table shows how various metrics may look like for an e-commerce solution development:

Program metrics	Engineering Metrics	Business metrics	Product metrics
Delivery milestone achievement	DORA metrics	Time spend on Key pages on website	Revenue increase from Digital journeys
Scope coverage	Scalability metrics	Marketing funnel ratio	Revenue increase from process improvements
Quality coverage	Tech Debt ratio	Click through Ratio	Cost savings from automation
Defect Density	RCA TAT	Product adoptions	NPS improvement

Diagram 21: The Key Digital Transformation Metrics

Each of these metrics, be it program, engineering, product, or business metrics, plays an important role. You may want to do a couple of weeks' workshop (if this is a brownfield project) to understand their lay of land and the current state of these metrics so that you can baseline them. This would also give an opportunity to define how to measure them during engagement between the two parties.

This model also provides an opportunity to forge a long-term partnership, since some of the metrics such as user's repeat visit, drop-off rate, conversion rate, product adoption, revenue increases through digital channels, etc., can only be measured 3-6 months after the solution has been put in the production.

Here is an illustration of a framework for an outcome-based model that can be used as an example for a large digital transformation program at a large insurance company:

Total Fee (TF) = Fixed Fee (FF) + Variable Fee (VF)

- FF is 70% of TF and is based on project milestones.
- VF is 30% of TF and is based on the target value achievement of various KPIs mentioned in the table below.

Metric	Theme, weights		KPI, weights		Baseline	Target
Product	*Engagement*	*10%*	*Average time spent on product page*	*25%*	*1 min*	*3 min*
			Self-serve premium renewal	*75%*	*25%*	*80%*
Business	*Revenue*	*35%*	*No of prospects reaching payment page*	*50%*	*10%*	*50%*
			No of x-sell/up-sell	*50%*	*20%*	*70%*
	Cost reduction	*25%*	*% calls in call centre*	*70%*	*80%*	*40%*
			Underwriting TAT	*30%*	*3 days*	*6 hrs*
Engineering	*Agility*	*10%*	*Deployment frequency*	*75%*	*Quarterly*	*Fortnight*
	Observability	*10%*	*Mean Time to Restore*	*25%*	*4 hrs*	*15 min*
Program	*Scope*	*10%*	*Scope coverage with no CR*	*100%*	*80%*	*90%*

Diagram 22: The Key Digital Transformation Metrics - An Illustrative Example

VF payout calculation can be linked with weighted average achievement of KPIs as per below table:

Outcome-based model

Achievement level	Risk and Reward
Suboptimal KPI achievement (< 70%)	VF* 0
Partial KPI achievement (70-95%)	VF*.8
Full KPI achievement (95-110%)	VF* 1
Exceed KPI achievement (110-140%)	VF* 1.3
Super-exceed KPI achievement (140- 180%)	VF* 1.6

Diagram 23: Variable Payout Calculation Framework - An Illustrative example

To sum it up, if partners are invited to a competitive bid and technology services in the RFPs (Request for proposals) are aligned to partner's long-term strategy, they should try coming up with outcome-based commercial proposals.

A few principles that need to be applied before considering this option are:

- You must have a deep understanding of the client's industry domain. Therefore, a partner's domain expertise is the most important criterion for proposing and succeeding with this model.The outcome creation must be measured using quantifiable data, so transparency in the "how to measure" process must be in place.

- Risks and rewards are determined by the success of specific goals or KPIs, which means pricing models must take care of both the upside and downside of goal achievement.

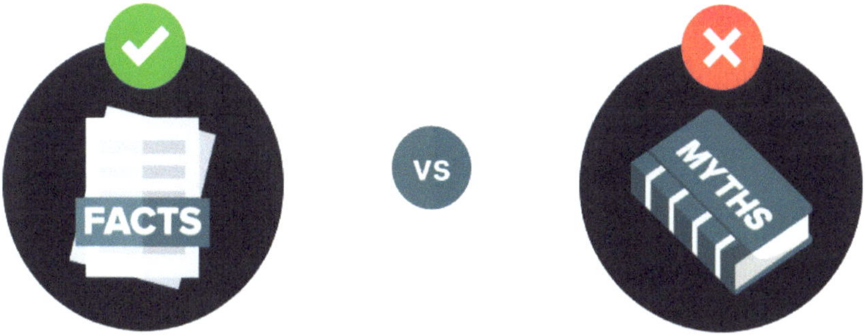

Diagram 24: Common Myths about Fixed Bid Programs

5.4 Common myths about Fixed Bid programs

When it comes to Fixed Bid commercial models, I've noticed a common discomfort among both clients and partners. This uneasiness often stems from varying interpretations of how Fixed Bid programs operate. These differing perspectives are typically shaped by experiences in the traditional waterfall approach and lack of exposure to evolving agile methodologies. I'd like to share my perspective on some of these interpretations, drawing from firsthand experiences.

1. Fixed Bid Transformation Programs Are Waterfall..ish in Nature!

Let's go back to the basics. Clients approach you with a business problem they need to solve, and technology is a key enabler in that process. When they choose you as a partner, it's because they believe in your solution, capabilities, and approach. They may not have a set methodology to reach their goals, so if your solution requires agile methods to iterate, test, and scale, it's your job to convince them. If you can clearly explain the benefits of your approach and share examples from past successes, they're likely to be open to trying it out.

However, some teams take a more rigid approach, quickly dismissing the client's current methods as inadequate. In the early stages of a partnership, when trust hasn't yet been built, this can create friction and set the project up for failure–often leading to misplaced blame on the contracting model.

Caselet 4

"I remember working with a mid-sized financial institution on a transformation program where the client wanted two weeks of User Acceptance Testing (UAT) after each incremental build in a Fixed Bid setup. However, we had planned for continuous UAT by the client's team throughout the development, with a four-week UAT period for each production build. This approach was not only more efficient but also significantly faster.

The trade-off was clear: Having one dedicated client stakeholder throughout the development life cycle for pairing with the partner's testing team (as a part of continuous UAT) versus saving two months for a faster Time to Market (TTM). .

After a few rounds of meaningful conversations, the clients were convinced by this trade-off and aligned with our proposed approach."

So, my advice is not to make assumptions in a new relationship or to jump to conclusions. By engaging in an open-minded discussion, you're much more likely to find a common path that works for both sides.

2. T&M is easier to execute because it has less cost pressure

In my experience, business and IT stakeholders in any enterprise work with budgets that are aligned and approved by the CFO

(Chief Finance Office) through a Cost and Benefit Analysis (CBA). This process evaluates each project's business benefits over the digital asset's shelf life, comparing them against the Total Cost of Ownership (TCO). The decision regarding the contracting model, whether Fixed Bid or Time & Materials (T&M), typically comes much later during the partner evaluation phase.

Regardless of the contracting model, every project team is committed to delivering the agreed-upon scope that meets business expectations. The execution methodology and its challenges aren't tied to the contracting model. Partners shouldn't assume that T&M contracts offer easy access to funds. Missing deadlines brings equal pressure in both contracting arrangements. If additional features are genuinely needed, both teams must agree on the necessity and potential for additional funding. However, if the partner team is at fault, the client may refuse to pay extra, and the partner may have to absorb the additional costs.

Caselet 5

"I remember a scenario during a transformational program where we were building a new product from scratch. The client's CTO had set the expectation that the budget allocated was already capped, and the market launch date had been decided. In this case, the commercial agreement was T&M.

After a couple of months, when our first release (MVP) was not promising enough to be tested in the market, the entire pressure of catching up to build those features, so that it could be tested well in the market, came upon us (partner team). ***Despite*** *the* ***T&M model, we had to incur costs*** *(additional people for 3-4 months) to ensure we were on track. The same CTO was used to look at every month's team timecards and ask tough questions about the value being delivered before approving the Monthly bill."*

3. **Fixed Bid program guarantees a fixed price for the customer**

This interpretation of Fixed Bid programs can often cause apprehension among partners, leading them to hesitate or even avoid committing to Fixed Bid engagements. Rarely is there a Fixed Bid program where the client does not incur additional costs due to changes in requirements, missed dependencies, or unforeseen challenges.

In my professional experience as a servicing partner, over 80% of the programs I managed involved change requests or adjustments stemming from missed dependencies. These situations typically led to meaningful discussions about the impact on costs. More often than not, we (the partners) were compensated for the extra effort, although it usually involved tough negotiations. Later in my career, when I transitioned to a client role, I applied this experience by negotiating with senior leadership to secure an additional 15-20% in funding on top of the transformational program budget. This contingency fund was carefully reserved for handling 'Change Requests' and other unforeseen needs.

Yes, it's true that every client expects their partner team to be highly proactive in managing risks and dependencies, with a strong aversion to cost escalations. A successful partner team is one that masters the art and science of setting clear boundaries for each scope item, allowing them to effectively manage legitimate change requests and persuade clients to pay for the additional effort. This tension between client and partner is a normal and accepted part of the relationship.

Caselet 6

"In one of my past engagements, we (the partner team) were tasked with understanding brand positioning, creating user personas, and defining the user experience layer for the client's new integrated digital assets–all within two months. Following this, we were

expected to proceed with content creation, feature development, and delivering a world-class experience using the underlying new CMS technology over the next ten months.

However, after three months, the team had only achieved 50% of the goals. Upon further investigation, it became evident that excessive deliberation on brand architecture and UX principles, along with multiple approval layers, had led to inefficiencies and process overheads, negatively impacting the commercial viability of the engagement.

A change request (CR) was initiated, presenting all relevant data. The negotiation took over two weeks, with multiple rounds of data scrutiny presented to the clients. Finally, the decision was made to compensate us (the partner team) for our effort loss. The CR was legitimized, and both sides recognized the need to be accountable for their responsibilities during program execution. Ultimately, ***the program was realigned on both fronts; cost and timeline.****"*

4. A Fixed Bid program ensures on-time delivery

Fixed Bid programs can create positive pressure on both sides of the team to give their best attempt to achieve their goals faster within the given constraints.

In technology services, the price generally reflects the estimated effort required to complete the project. Ideally, if there are no changes, risks, or missed dependencies, the effort estimate should stay within the same ballpark range, and the project should be delivered on time. However, reality often differs. Changes and risks impact effort estimates and timelines.

In a Fixed Bid program, the project manager's key role is to identify and mitigate risks, manage dependencies, and handle changes. **When a change arises, the PM should verify its legitimacy, present it to the Change Control Board with a thorough impact**

analysis, and keep everyone updated on the revised plan. The PM's responsibility is to ensure all stakeholders are aware of and accountable for changes, risks, and missed dependencies.

Caselet 7

I clearly remember the day when my project manager (from the partner's team) first reported missed API dependencies from the client's ESB team in our complex tech transformation program, which was running on a Fixed Bid basis.

With an ***18-month program and a pre-agreed go-live date****, every intermediate milestone was critical. We were only in the second month of execution, and I was well aware of the complexities of working with the client's IT organization, which involved coordinating with four different teams: Digital (for front-end development), ESB (for APIs), Enterprise Architecture (for DataBase and architecture), and Marketing (for UX design approval). Managing this was no easy task for the PM.*

I reached out to the CIO and proposed a joint workshop to identify all dependencies across the teams. While most teams began meeting their commitments, the ESB team continued to fall short. When the PM reported a second missed deadline, we probed further and discovered that the ESB team was running three months behind on provisioning API signatures.

After three rounds of tough negotiations, ***we had to revise the plan and push the go-live date*** *to align with the ESB team's readiness. As a result, we (the partner team) had to adjust staffing to avoid margin loss during this extended delay.*

5. Fixed Bid program = unlimited changes for clients

In today's software development landscape, requirements cannot be fully defined upfront; they evolve iteratively. Initially, both parties agree on a high-level scope, with details being refined over time. During execution, changes are inevitable, whether they involve adjusting scope boundaries or adding new elements. In my experience, over 95% of projects see clients requesting changes like logic adjustments, new features, additional validations, or new integrations. Missed dependencies can also increase effort and shift timelines.

However, the partner does not have to absorb all these changes without compensation. It often involves negotiating trade-offs. Lower-priority scope items may be swapped out to accommodate changes, but typically, a strong change request process is required. Minor changes might be handled with minimal process overhead, but major changes need thorough assessment for impact, effort, and cost. These changes should be communicated and approved before being developed.

Caselet 8

In a complex application migration program, our partner team was tasked with understanding the architecture of six existing applications and adapting them to fit the target cloud architecture within a 10-month timeframe. We developed a high-level understanding during a 4-week discovery phase, after which a fixed fee for the entire migration was agreed upon, along with a non-negotiable migration date. The client's on-premise data center vendor imposed a significant penalty for missing this deadline.

The program began positively, but three months in, we encountered numerous changes. Some of these were due to a lack of understanding of the architectural complexities and new requirements for integrating the applications into the cloud ecosystem. These changes had not been anticipated during the discovery phase.

The situation became complicated with ongoing back-and-forth discussions to determine the necessary adjustments. Our team struggled to establish effective governance for decision-making and change request management. We escalated these issues to the steering committee, presenting a detailed analysis of the changes discussed, their impact on the project, and associated costs. All changes were evaluated using the ***MOSCOW*** *framework (Must-have, Should-have, Could-have, and Won't-have). Through trade-off discussions, many changes were dropped due to the* ***trade-off between lower customer value and higher business costs****.*

This intervention led to a streamlined process for managing further change requests. After negotiating cost adjustments and putting in extra work over weekends, we successfully met the deadlines and avoided the potential cut-over delay penalty for our client.

This experience highlighted that a Fixed Bid program does not equate to unlimited changes. Ultimately, we celebrated the successful cut-over to production.

6. T&M needs more client involvement, but Fixed Price does not

In Time & Materials (T&M) projects, clients typically take the lead, especially in staff augmentation or co-sourced delivery setups. For T&M projects with multiple vendors, having a client-side program manager is essential to manage team utilization and resolve intra-team dependencies, making the client more accountable for day-to-day deliveries and issue resolution.

However, client involvement is equally crucial in Fixed Bid engagements. Fixed Bid programs often have aggressive timelines, and meeting the agreed scope within the set timeframe is a challenge from the start. The partner team's project manager cannot drive the program to completion without close collaboration with key client stakeholders. This includes managing risks, finalizing solution approaches, obtaining sign-offs on key deliverables, and resolving daily issues and dependencies.

In my experience, successful transformation programs - regardless of the contracting arrangement - require a strong partnership between both the teams. Co-creation through effective collaboration often leads to the best results.

Chapter 6

Executing Digital Transformation within Constraints

6.0 How to Execute Large Digital Transformation Programs

We've established a shared understanding of how technology has evolved over the past 30 years and how this evolution has shaped software development methodologies. We've also explored the mental models of key decision-makers and various contracting models supporting their thought process. Along the way, we've encountered perceptions and myths that can hinder embracing the strengths of one model over another. Now it's time to dive into the recipe for a successful digital transformation program.

But before we delve into the details, let's acknowledge the reality:

Executing any digital transformation program is full of challenges.

Many of you must have experienced some of the following challenges:

- **Vision and Goals Lost in Execution:** Many transformation programs start with a strong vision and clear goals, but these often get lost during execution, leading to misalignment across teams. Frequently, the absence of proper methods to measure benefits creates challenges in tracking ROI.

- **Ecosystem Complexity and Integration Challenges:** The complexity of integrating new digital solutions with existing systems and processes is often underestimated, leading to significant technical and operational hurdles.

- **Managing Dependencies:** Coordinating across multiple teams, partners, and technologies can lead to bottlenecks, especially when dependencies are not clearly identified and managed. Weak program management and governance can result in significant delays in addressing intra-team dependencies.
- **Change Management:** Digital transformation programs often require changes to established processes, technologies, or mindsets, which can face significant resistance from stakeholders. Ensuring all stakeholders are aligned and that changes are effectively communicated and adopted is critical but challenging.
- **Change Request Management:** As the program advances, there may be pressures to add new features or requirements, leading to scope expansion and change requests (CRs). Managing these requests becomes even more complex within existing commercial constraints and timelines.
- **Data Quality and Governance:** Poor data quality or inadequate data governance can hinder decision-making during program execution, negatively impacting the overall effectiveness of digital initiatives

Over the past 25 years in technology, I've encountered many challenges that often arise in digital transformation programs. Starting as an AS/400 developer, moving into consulting, and later working on digital transformation strategies, I've dealt with the complexities of technology integration, managing dependencies, and driving change across industries. From development to scaling and managing digital assets, these experiences have taught me that while challenges are inevitable, they can be managed with the right approach, leading to the best possible outcomes.

So, what does this approach look like? Can it help you win some of the challenges?

6.1 Winning Recipe for a Large Transformation Program

Let's explore the **key ingredients** for a winning recipe in a successful digital transformation program.

6.1.1. **Agree** on the Winning Theme

6.1.2. **Develop** a Shared Understanding of Program Goals and Scope

6.1.3. **Baseline** Scope with Boundaries at the Earliest

6.1.4. **Align** on Ways of Working

6.1.5. **Approach** Estimating and Planning Pragmatically

6.1.6. **Understand** Trade-offs Carefully

6.1.7. **Articulate** Delivery Value on a Continuous Basis

6.1.1 Agree on the Winning Theme

We often think of success as a win-win situation between the client and partner stakeholders, Typically, these stakeholders can be charaterized as:

Client Leadership:

- Business Owner, Engineering Owner, Product Owner
- Success Metrics: Revenue growth, customer retention, NPS, DORA metrics, tech debt, product adoption, and digital penetration.
- They're considered successful when these metrics improve.

Partner Leadership:

- Account Lead, Delivery Lead, Technology Lead
- Success Metrics: Annual recognized revenue (ARR), CSAT score, and program profitability.
- They're successful when these metrics show positive results.

But there's often a missing stakeholder: **The Project Team.**

I've seen large transformation programs where the project team across both teams (Project Managers, Business Analysts, Tech Leads, Developers, Quality Engineers , DevOps, UX designers, etc.) worked under immense pressure with little psychological safety, learning opportunities, or career growth. While the program might achieve short-term goals, it often struggles in the long-term due to team dissatisfaction and high attrition.

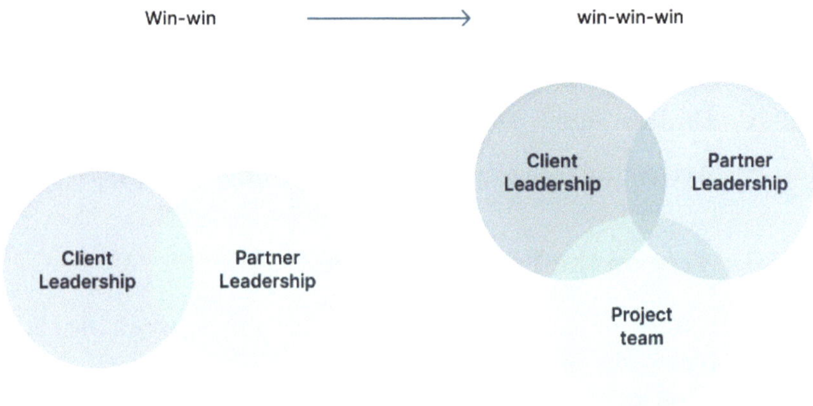

Diagram 25: Win-Win-Win model of a Large Transformation Program

The project team's success might include:

- Team engagement, individual motivation
- Career growth, learning opportunities
- Work-life balance, physical and psychological safety

In large transformation programs with many constraints, client and partner leadership must ensure a healthy environment where the KPIs of all three stakeholders are monitored and balanced and the transformation is truly sustainable for the long term. Only then can we achieve **a true win-win-win**.

6.1.2 Develop a shared understanding of program goals and scope

Diagram 26: Shared understanding of Program Goals and Scope

In any large transformation program, each stakeholder may have different goals and expectations, making it crucial for the partner team to establish a shared understanding of the program's goals and scope. This initial agreement should be documented as the baseline scope and protected with clear boundaries (even at a high level), so everyone knows when those boundaries are being crossed. While getting buy-in from all stakeholders can be challenging and time-consuming, it's essential and takes about **1-3 weeks** depending upon the size and complexity of the engagement. And it is **totally worth it**.

Remember, every program starts as an idea to meet a business need. Business stakeholders collaborate with technology and digital teams to assess the idea's feasibility and benefits through a Cost-Benefit Analysis (CBA).

During the RFP (Request for Proposal) stage, client stakeholders outline the initiative and its scope, shaped by the CBA. The partner team must capture this knowledge and transition it to the development or delivery team. This stage, known as pre-discovery scope alignment, involves aligning goals, modules/features, key use cases and personas, and sometimes even high-level customer journeys. Understanding constraints like timelines, market roll-out dates, and third-party dependencies further helps to understand the big picture.

Let's take a case study to understand these concepts slightly better.

Case Study: Transforming Apex Health Insurance's Customer Experience: Apex Health Insurance, a mid-sized regional health insurance provider, is facing stiff competition from digital-first competitors. To remain competitive and improve customer satisfaction, Apex has decided to undergo a digital transformation program focused on revamping its customer experience by modernizing its customer portal and mobile app.

The proposal team is expected to understand the program goals, capture the program scope during the RFP stage, and transition it to the delivery team if the work is awarded to your firm.

Case study – Apex Health Insurance

Metric	Type	Existing	Target	Measurement
Customer Retention Rate	Business	75%	85%	Percentage of customers retained annually
Net Promoter Score (NPS)	Business	20	40	Score on a scale of -100 to +100
Digital Engagement Rate	Product	60%	80%	% of active users engaging with digital channel
Digital Penetration Rate	Product	50%	70%	% of target market using the digital product
Deployment cycle	Engineering	8 weeks	4 weeks	Production release frequency

Diagram 27: Case Study - Program Metrics

Try capturing program goals representing all client stakeholders (business, product, and engineering team). It's crucial to understand how clients measure these metrics, the frequency of measurement, and what other factors influence them. It's beneficial to ask for deeper

Case study – Apex Health Insurance

Module	Description	Integration/ New development	Screens & Complexity	Process Re-engineering	Scope Boundary
Customer Portal	Modernized web interface for managing policies and claims	New Development	10 screens (High)	Yes	Scope includes redesign of existing portal only; excludes backend integration and legacy data migration
Mobile App	Updated app for policy management and notifications	New Development	8 screens (Medium)	Yes	Scope covers redesign for iOS and Android apps; excludes additional platform support and extensive new features.
User Authentication	Secure login and identity verification	Integrate with existing system	N/A (Integration)	No	Integration with current SSO system; no overhaul of authentication protocols.
Claims Management	Streamlined process for managing insurance claims	New Development	6 screens (Medium)	Yes	Scope includes new UI/UX for claims management; excludes back-end processing and legacy claims data handling
Customer Support	Integrated support features (chat, email, phone)	New Development	5 screens (Medium)	Yes	Scope includes new support interface; excludes major changes to existing support workflows.
Personalized Dashboard	Customizable dashboard for key information	New Development	4 screens (Medium)	No	Scope covers creation of a new dashboard interface; excludes advanced analytics and integration with external data sources.
Notifications & Alerts	Notifications & Alerts	Integrate with existing system	N/A (Integration)	No	Integration with current notification system; excludes development of new notification
Data Analytics	Analysing customer behaviour and feedback	New Development	7 screens (High)	Yes	Scope includes new analytics dashboards; excludes advanced data modelling and third-party analytics tools integration.
Integration Services	Connects with backend systems and third-party services	Integrate with existing system	N/A (Integration)	No	Integration with existing back-end systems; excludes development of new API endpoints or third-party integrations.

Diagram 28: Case Study - High Level Scope

data behind these metrics so that the partner team can assess how much of this can be impacted by modernizing the customer portal and improving the customer experience through digital channels.

In some RFP situations, partners might not have the chance to conduct workshops but can still clarify scope and boundary conditions through common Q&A forums.

6.1.3 Baseline Scope with Boundaries at the Earliest (Discovery):

Before you begin your discovery workshops with clients, ensure that you have gathered all the relevant information from your pursuit team and thoroughly reviewed the artifacts created during that stage. This will help you understand the customer's problem and their pain points.

Baselining scope starts with creating a common visual reference of the solution you are proposing to solve their problem. One method I strongly recommend is to create **high to mid-level user journeys, followed by low-fidelity wireframes** for each use case. Low-fidelity wireframes provide the information architecture of the user's interactions with the proposed solution, showcasing interaction design and key calls to action (CTAs). This approach not only helps in understanding the solution faster but also reduces the processing overhead of creating lengthy, abstracted scope documentation. Here is an example of such a visual journey.

Next comes the creation of **the Solution Work Breakdown Structure (WBS)**, also known as product backlog in Agile methodologies. This WBS should ideally capture scope at the epic or story level, depending on what is feasible within the given timeframe and context. It helps establish clear guardrails to help carve out a scope boundary.

Here is an example of a Solution WBS (Work Breakdown Structure) for the above case study. The solution WBS template may include

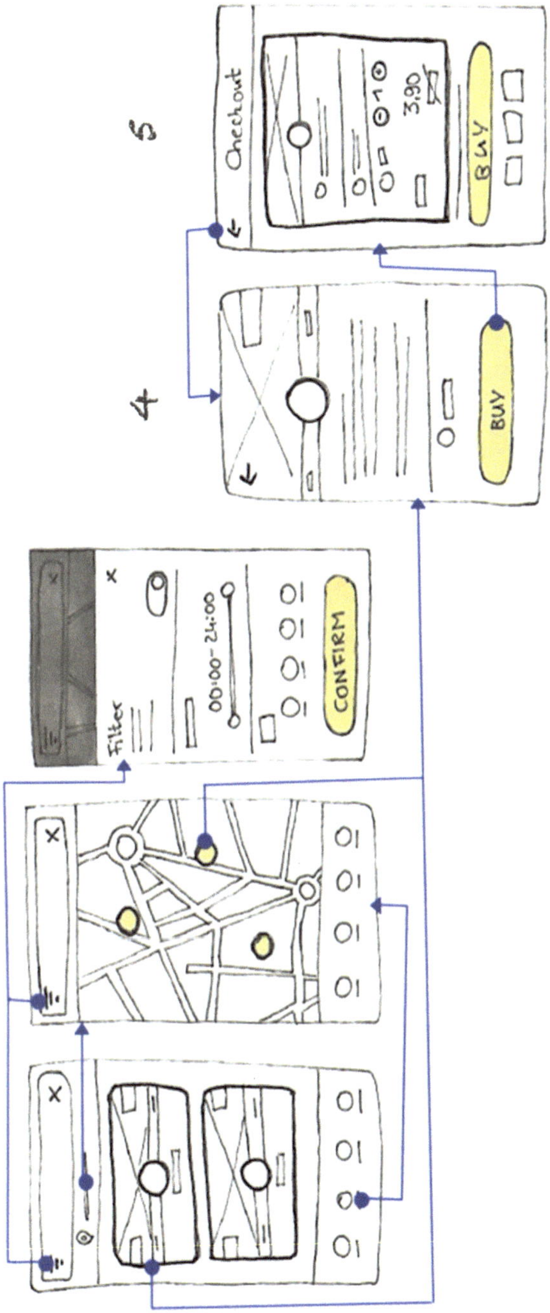

Diagram 29: Low Fidelity Concepts - An Illustrative Example

Solution WBS – Apex Health

Module	Solution Epics	Stories	Solution Boundaries	Tech Assumptions
Customer Portal	- User Account Management - Policy Information Access - Claims Tracking - Customer Support	- As a user, I want to register and log in to my account. - As a user, I want to view my policy details. - As a user, I want to track my claim status. - As a user, I want to contact customer support via chat.	- Integrate with existing policy management systems - Limited to web-based access - Excludes backend policy processing	- Web technologies (React, Angular) - Cloud hosting - API integrations with existing systems
Mobile App	- User Registration and Login - Policy Viewing - Claims Submission - Notifications	- As a user, I want to register and log in to the mobile app. - As a user, I want to view my policy details on my phone. - As a user, I want to submit a claim through the app. - As a user, I want to receive push	- Sync with Customer Portal - Mobile-specific UI/UX design - Excludes advanced analytics	- Native mobile development (iOS, Android) - Push notification services - Mobile backend services
Claims Processing	- Automated Claims Intake - Claims Approval Workflow - Claims Status Tracking	- As a claim's processor, I want to automatically intake claims. - As a claim's processor, I want to review and approve claims. - As a user, I want to track the status of my claim. - As a manager, I want to generate claims status reports.	- Integration with existing claims database - Excludes manual claim handling - Limited to automated processes	- Workflow automation tools - Claims management system APIs - Secure cloud storage
Customer Support System	- Ticket Management - Live Chat Support - FAQ Management	- As a user, I want to create a support ticket. - As a user, I want to chat live with a support agent. - As a user, I want to browse frequently asked questions. - As a support agent, I want to manage and respond to tickets.	- Integration with existing CRM system - Excludes telephone support - Focus on digital channels	- CRM integration - Chatbot technology - Knowledge base management
Analytics and Reporting	- Customer Interaction Analytics - Claims Reporting - Performance Dashboards	- As a manager, I want to view analytics on customer interactions. - As a manager, I want to generate reports on claims. - As a manager, I want to see performance dashboards. - As a user, I want to access self-service reporting tools.	- Data pulled from Customer Portal and Claims Processing - Excludes in-depth business intelligence - Focus on key metrics	- Data visualization tools (Tableau, Power BI) - Real-time data processing

Diagram 30: Case Study - Solution WBS

many other details such as complexity, priority, etc., depending on the project's needs.

I also prefer capturing some program-level scope and assumptions, such as the number of user personas this solution may cater to and the number of people for each persona that the team will interview to understand their digital behavior (especially if it's a UX-heavy engagement). Similarly, the number of internal and external applications to be integrated, the number of APIs involved, their complexity, and the methods of integration (e.g., SOAP, REST, XML).

A sample of such **program-level assumptions** can be objectively captured like this. This is just a sample list for the purpose of illustration, not a comprehensive list.

Program level assumption

Category	Program Assumptions
UX research	- User Interviews to be conducted in 5 cities for 3 user persona - Max 25 interviews (across 5 cities, 5 people per user persona)
UX design	- Wires and visual designs will undergo max 2 rounds of review cycle - Feedback to be provided to partner's team within a weeks' time
API integrations	- 20-25 APIs tom be integrated - All APIs to be provisioned in REST/XMK format - API signature to be made available in Dev/QA environment a week before Dev Sprints
UAT (user acceptance testing)	- User acceptance testing will be a continuous process along with partner's QA team - 2 weeks of UAT is included in the plan for each production release
Back-end integrations	- Back-end system such as Claims, policy management, CRM will be integrated to fetch the data from the respective system - No development of backend system is included as part of this program - If there is any new functionality is to be re-written in the back-end program needs to be synced with this program plan - Existing business logic will be leveraged for automative claim review and approval.
Analytics and Reporting	- Existing data visualisation tool will be used for data visualisation and reports and license will be provided by client for such need - Only real data processing will be considered for agreed reports - Number of screens for data visualisation are limited to 5 and 15 key reports will be supported as part of this program
Data migration	- Client data team to provision data to the partner team for integration testing. However, Data migration to the production is not part of this program

Diagram 31: Case Study - Program Assumptions

To sum up, the discovery process should be approached with objectivity and pragmatism. The goal is to gather as much information as possible to establish a baseline scope, create boundaries, and right-size the efforts. This approach helps identify any deviations from the initial program understanding. In case of any surprise, present the facts with supporting details to the program leadership team. This may be the first challenging situation for leadership to address, and handling it with ease involves aligning on common interests, making necessary re-prioritizations, and considering trade-offs. I've found that such conversations often lead to positive outcomes.

6.1.4 Align on ways of working

To ensure everyone is aligned on the daily and weekly operations of the program, it's important to agree on the following: the methods and practices we'll use, any dependencies we need to manage, the sign-off process, and how we'll handle change requests. This alignment will help keep things consistent and keep the program running smoothly.

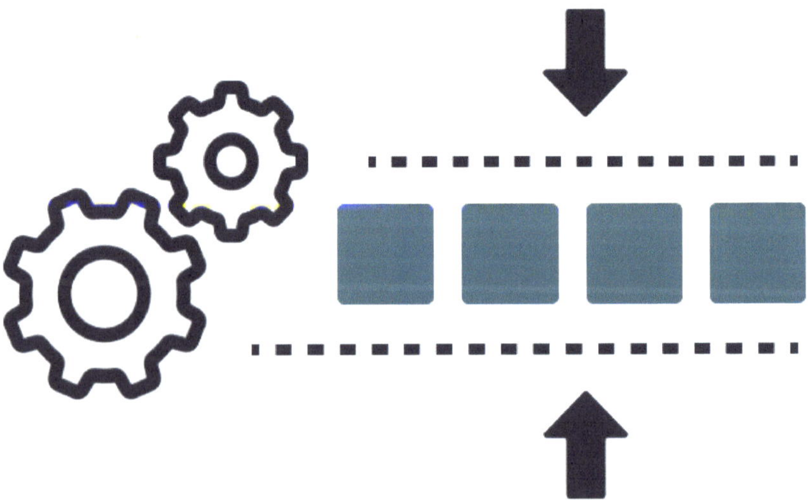

Diagram 32: Align on Ways of Working

1. **Methodology, Practices & Ceremonies**

Methodology

- Avoid clinging too tightly to past experiences or preconceived beliefs about methodologies. Instead, foster a safe space where everyone can listen to each other's stories and identify common elements that resonate with the entire team.
- Don't label it as strictly waterfall or agile. It could be a unique version of Hybrid.
- If possible, ask the team to vote for a creative name. It will have more of a sense of belonging.

Practices

- Establish clear guidelines for both synchronous and asynchronous communication. Asynchronous communication enhances thought clarity and provides time for deep thinking, ultimately increasing productivity. Meanwhile, synchronous communication is important for debottlenecking and resolving intra-team dependencies and blockers.
- Align on pairing practices, whether it's developer pairing or cross-functional pairing. Pairing improves the onboarding time, facilitates code reviews, and promotes knowledge sharing. At times, partner and client team member pairing helps build the story context faster and in the long-term builds trust as well.
- Be thoughtful on who should be part of which meeting. Choose the person who is directly contributing to the meetings.
- Status or progress updates may be managed asynchronously.
- Create an environment of inclusivity and experiments.

Ceremonies

- Facilitate a workshop to come up with those ceremonies that matter the most to your people.

Internal and External Dependencies – Case Study

Dependency	Description	Tentative resolution week	Team owner
Integration APIs	Provision of APIs to access current policy management, claims processing, and customer support systems for integration	Week 4 onwards	Integration team
Design approval	Availability of client's stakeholders for necessary brainstorming and approval of wires and visual design etc	Week 4 onwards	Product and Marketing team
Technical resources	Access to client's IT team for system integration, technical support, and troubleshooting	Week 2	IT Helpdesk
Security Requirements	Client's security protocols and compliance requirements that must be adhered to during development.	Week 4	Security & Compliance Team
User Acceptance Testing (UAT)	Availability of client's UAT team to perform testing and validate functionalities throughout the dev cycle	Ongoing (Throughout project)	Client's Quality Assurance Team
Infrastructure Access	Provision and access to client's infrastructure for deployment and testing of new solutions	Week 5	Infrastructure Team
Third-Party Services	Coordination with third-party services or vendors that are integrated into the new system such as CRM, Payment gateway etc	Week 8 onwards	Client PM
Data Availability	Availability of accurate and up-to-date policy, claims, and customer data for testing the integrations	Week 3	Enterprise Data team

Diagram 33: Case Study - Dependency Matrix

- Always look for the purpose of the meeting and drop, continue, or alter ceremonies based on how much the purpose is being achieved.
- Daily stand ups, iteration showcases, iteration retrospection, product prioritization, change request (CR) trade-offs, risk reviews, program governance, etc., seem to be good candidates.
- Don't be too dogmatic about all the ceremonies. Sometimes a team's maturity can be a legit criteria to add or drop a specific ceremony.

2. Dependencies

A large, complex transformation program may have multiple dependencies that need to be managed proactively. Creating a list of these dependencies with tentative closure dates and identified owners during the early phases of the program helps in managing the critical path effectively. Here is an illustration of dependencies for the case study (not the comprehensive list).

3. Sign-off matrix

In a complex ecosystem, key stakeholders often need to make timely decisions across various aspects of the program. This may include approvals for items such as wireframes, visual design, API contracts, critical business logic, technical architecture, and environment specifications. To manage this efficiently, it's essential to identify the stakeholders responsible for these sign-offs and document them in a sign-off matrix. Establishing a lightweight cadence for managing these sign-offs helps ensure that approvals are obtained promptly, keeping the project on track.

In the sign-off matrix, client stakeholders provide the actual sign-offs, while the team owner is accountable for facilitating the process and ensuring that sign-offs are completed on time. It's important to set these expectations with all the stakeholders from the start.

Sign-off matrix– Case Study

Area/Item	Description	Key Stakeholders Responsible	Sign-off Deadline	Team owner Accountable
Wires and Visual Design	Approval of wireframes, UI/UX design, and overall visual aesthetics	UX Lead, Product Owner, Client CMO	Each design sprint (week4 onwards)	UX Design Team Lead
API Contracts	Finalizing API contracts for integration with existing systems and third parties.	Integration Lead, Tech Architect, Client CTO	Each Dev sprint (week 6 onwards)	Integration Team Lead
Critical Business Logic	Approval of core business logic, workflows, and rules.	Product Owner, Client CIO, Business Analysts	Dev -1 sprint (week 5 onwards)	Product Management Lead
Tech Architecture	Finalizing system architecture, including data flow, security, and environment specs.	Tech Architect, Client CTO	Week 4	Architecture Team Lead
Environment Specifications	Approval of environments for development, testing, and production.	DevOps Lead, Client IT Manager	Week 3	DevOps Team Lead
Security Requirements	Sign-off on security protocols, compliance measures, and risk management strategies	Security Lead, Client CISO	Week 4	Security Team Lead

Diagram 34: Case Study - Sign-off Matrix

4. Change request management

We often face challenges when implementing the change request management process.

First, it's common to view the process as cumbersome and conflict-prone, which can deter us, since most people prefer to avoid conflict. However, the key is to learn how to manage and resolve conflicts effectively, viewing them as a normal part of business. This requires a shift in mindset.

Second, awareness and discipline are crucial. Introducing a lightweight change request process early in the project, during the kick-off, helps mitigate surprises. Additionally, creating templates and assigning teams to handle different aspects of changes, one for effort and impact analysis and another for prioritization and approvals helps separate responsibilities and reduces system noise.

This lightweight process can be quite simple like the one below:

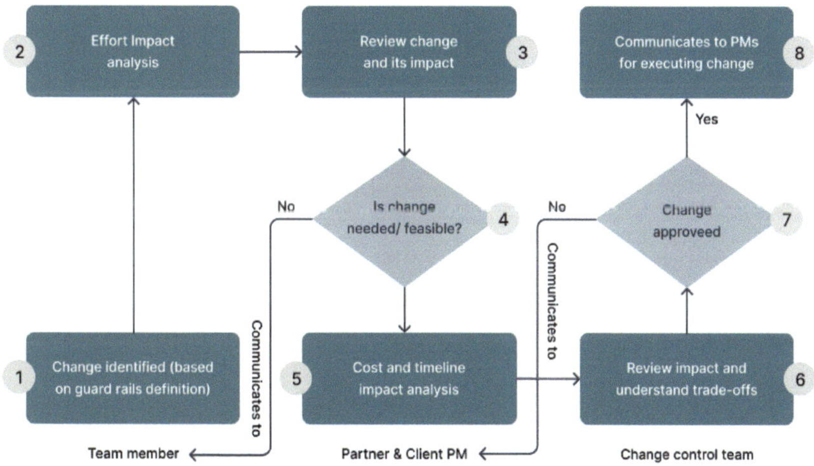

Diagram 35: An example of light weight Chane Request Management Process

- Team members may identify the 'Change' and initiate this with impact analysis.
- Project Managers (PMs, from either side) should align on the legitimacy of the change and further come up with the cost and timeline impact of the change before presenting it to the Change Control Leaders.
- The Change Control Leaders should review the change within the broader context of the program and apply trade-offs to decline the changes or approve it with additional funding (if needed).

6.1.4 Approach Estimating and Planning pragmatically

Diagram 36: A Pragmtic Approach towards Estimation and Planning

I have noticed many teams getting stressed over the estimates. Estimates are just informed guesses about what might happen - they're not meant to be precise. For big digital transformations, the goal of estimating during discovery is to get a good understanding of the scope at different levels, like epics or stories, and to see how confident the team is about completing the work. A simple approach to estimation and planning is to start with detailed bottom-up estimates, then do a top-down review, and finally reconcile the two.

Bottoms up estimation tool

Phase/ Module	Epic/Story	Assumption/ Boundary	Complexity	Optimistic effort (person days)	Pessimistic effort (person days)	Most Likely effort (person days)	Weightage average (person days)
Capture standard phases and functional epics	Wherever possible break down epics to stories	Associate phase, epic or stories to any risk, assumption. Create guard rails as much as possible	High/ Medium/ Low	Estimate with no risks	Estimate with maximum risks	Estimate with some risks occurring	(O+4M+P)/6
Discovery with 4 people for 3 weeks	Understanding business metrics, scope, tech landscape, stakeholders etc	Non availability of stakeholders, no system access to understand tech complexity, lack of documentations etc	High	60 =(4*3*5)	100 =(4*5*5)	80 =(4*4*5)	80
Tech Architecture with 2 people for 4 weeks	High to mid component level architecture	Go ahead to be obtained within 2 weeks	Medium	20 =(2*2*5)	30 =(2*3*5)	22 =(2*11)	23
UX Design with 2 people for 4 weeks	UX journey, wires and VDs	Design approval to be obtained within 3 weeks with 2 max iterations	Medium	20 =(2*2*5)	40 =(2*4*5)	30 =(2*3*5)	30
Customer portal	Implement user registration and login functionality	Web technologies (React, Angular) Cloud hosting API integrations with existing systems	High	10	16	14	14
	Develop policy detail's view		High	10	16	14	14
	Create claim status tracking		Medium	8	14	10	10
	Integrate chat support		High	10	16	14	14
Mobile App	Develop user registration and login for mobile	Sync with Customer Portal Mobile-specific UI/UX design Mobile backend services	Medium	8	14	10	10
	Implement policy details view on mobile		Medium	8	14	10	10
	Enable claims submission through the app		High	10	16	14	14
	Set up push notifications		Low	6	9	8	8
Claims Processing	Automate claims intake process	Workflow automation tools Claims management system APIs Secure cloud storage	Medium	8	10	8	8
	Develop claims approval workflow		High	10	16	14	14
	Implement claim status tracking		Low	6	8	7	7
	Create claims status reporting functionality		High	10	14	12	12
Customer Support System	Implement support ticket creation	Existing CRM integration API available Chatbot technology Knowledge base management	Medium	8	12	10	10
	Set up live chat functionality		High	10	16	14	14
	Develop FAQ management system		High	10	16	14	14
	Create ticket management for support agents		High	10	16	14	14
Analytics and Reporting	Develop customer interaction analytics	Data visualization tools (Tableau, Power BI Dev licenses are available with clients Only Real-time data processing Data migration is not part of scope	High	10	16	14	14
	Implement claims reporting functionality		High	10	16	14	14
	Create performance dashboards		High	10	16	14	14
	Set up self-service reporting tools		High	10	16	14	14
NFR	Load testing (2 rounds)	Load testing license product is available for max 500 concurrent users	High	10	16	14	14
	Security testing (2 rounds)	Client to provide licensed security testing tool Appscan	Medium	5	7	6	6
	API TPS testing (2 rounds)	Client to provide API testing tool	High	10	16	14	14
QA (E2E)	End to end functional testing for Pre-UAT scenario	25% of Dev effort	High	80	120	100	100
DevOps	CI/CD setup and prod deployment support	20% capacity of dev for Pipeline setup and continuous deployments	Medium	50	70	60	60
Final UAT support	Dev support for 2 weeks each for 3 production release	UAT to be time boxed and done for critical scenarios	Medium	60	80	70	70
						Total	687

Diagram 36: Case Study - Bottom-up Estimation

Bottom up estimates:

I like using the Program Evaluation and Review Technique (PERT) based bottoms-up estimates because it helps in capturing a range of possible outcomes. By considering optimistic, pessimistic, and most likely scenarios, PERT provides a weighted average estimate

Objective Risk Assessment Tool during estimation

Category	Objective Risks	Prob %	Description	Risk Buffer (in person days)	Multiplier	Total Risk Buffer (in person days)
Tech	Complex API integrations (Appx 10)	60%	3rd party contract may change during the discussion	5	10	30
	Non availability of load testing, security testing tool	50%	Client IT stakeholder may have many prioirties inside	5	2	5
	Non availability of pre-prod environment for various testing	50%	Cloud partner dependencies	5	1	2.5
UX design	Sign-off delays	70%	due to competing priorities and multiple layer of stakeholders	10	2	14
People	Unplanned sick leave/casual leave	100%	7 days in a year	3	7	21
	Rotation/Ramp up (3 people)	100%	5 days of productivity loss for every rotation	5	3	15
UAT Risks	Unavailability of UAT people	50%	Due to competing priorities in the org	10	2	20
					Total Risk Buffer	**107.5**

Diagram 37: Case Study - Risk Assessment

that balances different perspectives and helps manage uncertainties effectively. This approach is particularly useful for projects with a high degree of complexity or uncertainties generally found in large digital transformation programs. Here is an illustration of bottoms-up estimates for the same case study using PERT based estimation tool:

Risk Buffer:

It's a good practice to keep a separate risk register to track risks at each stage. Here is an example of an objective risk tool that may be used for capturing objective risks during the estimation process. The below risks are an illustration of the case study program.

Top-down estimates:

Experts usually estimate project duration, phases, and the team size based on their experience with similar work. If the project is similar to one done elsewhere, it's a good idea to bring in someone from outside the program for a more objective estimate. This method is known as 'analogous estimation' as it draws comparisons from the past projects to make predictions.

The following assumptions have been taken into consideration while creating the above top-down estimates:

- The discovery phase is planned for 3 weeks with a Tech Lead, Business Analyst, Project Manager, and UX Designer.
- The Tech Lead and UX roles will continue working on technology and UX design for another 2-3 weeks, whereas the Business Analyst (BA) should continue until the backlog is groomed.
- The project duration is set at six months, based on the client's goal to launch within that time frame.
- Development risks have been accounted for by appropriately staffing to address objective risks.

Role	W1	W2	W3	W4	W5	W6	W7	W8	W9	W12	W13	W14	W15	W16	W17	W18	W19	W20	W21	W22	W23	W24	W25	W26	Total
	Discovery			Design Tech+UX 1		Design Tech+UX 2																			
				Dev- i0		Dev- i1		Dev- i2		UAT Support		Dev-i3		Dev-i4		UAT Support		Dev-i5		Dev-i6		UAT Support			
										UAT 1		Prod				UAT 2		Prod				UAT 3		Prod	
TL	1	1	1	1	1	1	1																		35
BA	1	1	1	1	1	1	1	1	1	1	1	1													60
PM	1	1	1	1	1	1	1	1	1	1	1	1	1	1	1	1	1	1	1	1	1	1	1	1	120
UX		1	1	1	1	1																			25
UX				1	1	1	1																		20
Sr Dev		1	1	1	1	1	1	1	1	1	1	1	1	1	1	1	1	1	1	1	1	1	1	1	115
Sr Dev						1	1	1	1	1	1	1	1	1	1	1	1								60
Dev						1	1	1	1	1	1	1	1	1	1	1	1	1	1	1	1	1	1	1	95
Dev						1	1	1	1	1	1	1	1	1											45
Dev Risk											1	1	1	1	1	1	1	1							40
QE				1	1	1	1	1	1	1	1	1	1	1	1	1	1	1	1	1	1	1	1	1	105
QE																1	1	1	1						20
DevOps				0.5	0.5	0.5	0.5	0.5	0.5	0.5	0.5	0.5	0.5	0.5	0.5	0.5	0.5	0.5	0.5	0.5	0.5	0.5	0.5	0.5	52.5
Total PDs	15	25	25	38	38	53	48	38	38	38	43	43	38	38	33	38	38	33	28	23	23	23	23	23	**793**

Diagram 38: Case Study - Top down Estimation

Reconciliation:

Keep a few things in mind while doing reconciliation:

- Remember that we have to staff people for objective risks. Hence, add a risk buffer to the bottom-up estimates and match this to top-down team capacity and start the reconciling process.
- Individual phases (such as discovery, design, and development) efforts and capacity should match within the range of 10-15%.
- Keep fine-tuning the staffing (in the top-down approach) for each individual row until the overall effort and capacity matches within 5% range.

	Bottoms up estimate	Top down capacity
Discovery	80	55
UX + Tech design	100	95
Dev effort Including UAT suppport	347	400
QA	100	125
DevOps	60	52
Risk buffer	107	65
Reconcillation	794.0	792

Diagram 39: Case Study - Reconciliation between Top-down and Bottom-up estimates

In summary, these two types of estimates reflect different perspectives: the first focuses on the developer's view of epic/story development and testing, while the second offers an expert opinion on the overall duration and size of the engagement. If approached objectively, these estimates might reveal differing results. A significant gap (over 20%) between the two should prompt a brainstorming session within the team. This should be seen as an opportunity to align by adjusting story estimates or refining the top-down staffing and duration.

6.1.6 Understand Trade-offs carefully

Diagram 40: Understand Trade-offs

A trade-off is a situation where you must choose between two conflicting options, where gaining one thing might mean sacrificing something else. In other words, it's about making adjustments to balance different priorities or needs. Let me illustrate this with a few examples:

1. In a large digital transformation program, when you are chasing a deadline, encountering a Change Request (CR) may pose this situation.
    - Should you accept this CR and delay the launch date (Customer value),
    - Should you drop the CR and proceed with the pre-agreed date (Time to Market)?

2. What if CR is extremely critical and offers maximum customer value in this release? You may have to pick this, but you can't delay the launch date beyond a week. This creates another trade-off situation.

    - Negotiate with a few people in the partner's team to stretch their hours during the week and work over the upcoming weekend to complete it (People Morale) while still launching it within a week's time (Time to Market).
    - Or finish the core of this CR quickly (Speed) and reduce the testing phase (Quality).

3. As a program leader, if you had to choose between proceeding with a sub-optimal team for the discovery phase versus delaying the discovery kick-off by a month, what would you choose? You need to understand the trade-off here.

    - Delaying the discovery phase means pushing the entire project timeline back by a month (Time to Market).
    - On the other hand, kicking off the most critical phase of the project with a sub-optimal team may pose many other risks subsequently and may delay the project by a couple of months later (More Risks).

4. If you were to decide between the tech approach of using a native app or a responsive web approach for a product that requires many native features for stickiness.

    - On one hand, native apps will provide native features that may increase initial adoption of the app and yield early business benefits (Early adoption).
    - On the other hand, it may incur more cost in the upfront development. Some duplication build effort may be needed for iPhone and Android (Upfront cost).

Trade-offs

Trade-off	Understanding the Impact
Rapid Implementation vs. Compliance Adherence	Accelerating timelines may lead to potential non-compliance, resulting in legal and financial risks. Ensuring compliance can be resource-intensive, affecting speed and flexibility.
Cost Efficiency vs. Investment in Cutting-edge Technology	Cost efficiency might lead to reliance on outdated technologies, potentially reducing market competitiveness. Investing in cutting-edge technology can drive innovation but might strain budgets and require additional training and resources.
Scope Expansion vs. Budget Constraints	Expanding scope can lead to higher costs and potential project delays. Staying within budget might require cutting back on desired features or functionalities
Innovation vs. Risk Management	Innovation can provide a competitive edge but introduces new risks that must be carefully managed. Risk management ensures stability but might limit the ability to innovate and adapt to changing market demands

Diagram 41: Case Study - Trade-offs

You can't have the best of both worlds. As a program leader responsible for achieving program objectives, it's crucial to understand the trade-off carefully. This understanding will help you make tough decisions and find the balance that works best for your goals. Here are a few more trade-offs that can be encountered as part of execution of the case study.

6.1.7 Articulate delivery value on a continuous basis

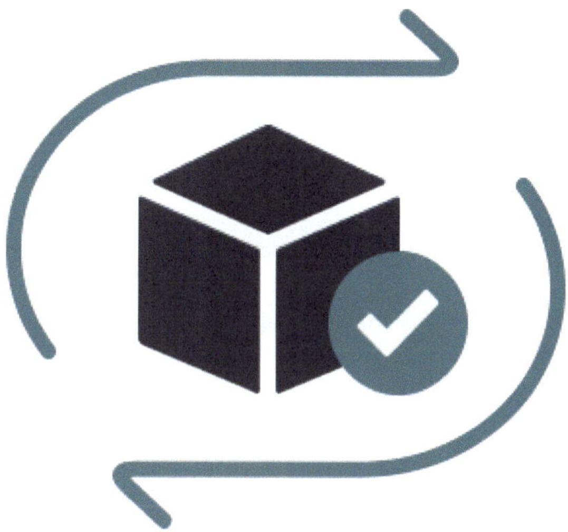

Diagram 42: Continuous Value Articulation

Articulating the delivery value on a continuous basis means regularly and clearly communicating the value that the project or program is delivering to stakeholders throughout its lifecycle. This involves consistently highlighting the benefits, progress, and impact of the work being done. By doing so, you ensure that all the stakeholders remain aligned with the project's objectives and understand how their investment is contributing to the overall goal.

Showcasing value begins with identifying the Value Realization Matrix, aligning stakeholders on their measurement methods.

Delivery			Engineering			Product			Business		
Metric	**Current**	**Target**	**Metric**	**Current**	**Target**	**Metric**	**Current**	**Target**	**Metric**	**Current**	**Target**
Delivery milestone achievement (timeline met)	*70%*	*90%*	*Deployment Freq*	*8 weeks*	*4 weeks*	*Digital engagement improvement*	*60%*	*80%*	*Customer retention ratio*	*75%*	*85%*
Scope coverage (Total scope delivered/Backlog agreed)	*80%*	*95%*	*Tech Debt ratio*	*15%*	*6%*	*Digital penetration improvement*	*50%*	*70%*	*Customer NPS Improvement*	*+20*	*+40*
Defect Density (Defects/ KLOC)	*.8*	*0.5*	*RCA TAT*	*48 hrs*	*18 hrs*	*Time spent on product pages*	*1 min*	*2.5 mins*	*Call centre load reduction due to self-serve feature*	*10K/m*	*30K/m*

Diagram 43: Case Study - Program Matrics Articulation - An Illustrative example

Establishing a baseline of the current state involves some due diligence, but it sets the foundation for tracking incremental progress over time.

Program Value Creation Dasboard			
Program Name	CX Trasnformation - Apex Health	**Start Date**	01/01/2025
Delivery Milestone	**MVP1** 24-Mar **MVP2** 5-May **Final Release** 20-Jun	**Planned Go Live**	20/06/2025
Delivery velocity	Show Delivery Velocity graph here = Iteration wise StoryPoints delivered & Comulative SPs	**Deplyement Frequency**	Graph showing Depl Freq for each build
Scope coverage	Backlog items covered per iteration/Total backlog items	**Build Failure Rate**	Graph showing Build Failure Rate for each build
Code coverage	% code covered by test cases (unit/integration/E2E test cases) by end of each build	**MTTR**	Graph showing MTTR for each build failure
Digital engagement rate	(Total active engagements/Total users)X100 weekly graph from MVP1 release onwards	**Customer Retention**	Customer retention improvement month by month after MVP1 release
Digital penetration rate	(Total active users/Total existing users for Apex)X100 weekly graph from MVP1 release onwards	**Call center load**	Call center load graph weekly chart after MVP1 release

Diagram 44: Program Dashboard Framework- An Illustrative example

I've noticed that many Program Dashboards focused solely on delivery progress, risks, and mitigation plans. While essential, this approach only addresses part of the picture. To genuinely demonstrate the value being created, I recommend establishing an additional dashboard that captures key value realization metrics. By doing so, the team can continuously articulate the value the program delivers. This not only keeps everyone aligned and transparent about the program's effectiveness but also fosters a sense of achievement within the team, boosting morale, and maintaining momentum. (A sample program value dashboard is provided above for reference).

6.2 How to set an engagement up for success!

Establishing an engagement requires careful consideration, as rushing to initiate a large transformation can introduce unnecessary risks. A well-thought-out setup is essential to pave the way for success!

Let's understand what we need to be aware of while setting up a large transformation program for win-win-win (see the definition of win-win-win in 6.1.1). Here is **a list of ten keypointers:**

6.2.1 A project well begun is a project half done!

A successful large transformation always starts with a strong discovery phase, built on great teamwork. This process works best when you have the right people in place, including a Business Analyst with deep knowledge, a Tech Analyst who focuses on details, and a Project Manager skilled in balancing both breadth and depth, orchestrating everything seamlessly. This is what makes a team truly great.

For programs with specific needs, it's critical to involve specialists: a hands-on DevOps expert for infrastructure-heavy projects or a User Research specialist for UX-driven initiatives.

Beyond technical skills, each member of the team must embody key attributes: empathy towards the client's needs, assertiveness to drive decisions, and a proactive mindset to stay ahead of challenges.

I'd much prefer delaying a project by a month to assemble the ideal team rather than rushing in with a less-than-optimal one. Remember, taking the time to set things up properly from the start prevents bigger issues down the line. A stitch in time truly saves nine.

To ensure the success of this complex transformation program, it's important to have the discovery team located closer to the client - ideally onshore. This phase isn't just about gathering project details; it's about building a strong relationship and trust with the client, which is crucial for long-term success.

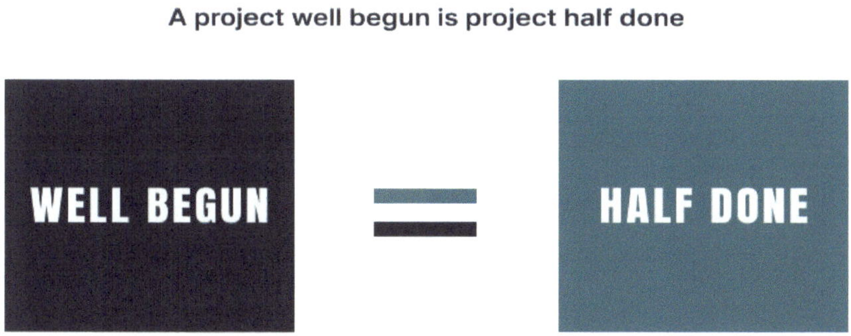

Diagram 45: Well Begun is Half Done

Being on-site allows us to establish trust more effectively through face-to-face interactions, fostering deeper connections and enabling quicker decision-making. It also allows for real-time collaboration, which helps resolve issues faster and aligns expectations early on, thereby avoiding costly delays down the line.

I also suggest committing to keeping the core discovery team - comprising the Business Analyst, Tech Analyst, and Project Manager - on board for at least a year. This continuity is essential for maintaining stability and ensuring the team understands both the client's needs and the program's evolving challenges. Having a consistent team will help avoid gaps in knowledge and potential disruptions as the program progresses.

By investing in this approach, we're setting the stage up for a successful discovery phase and building long-term trust and stability. This will ultimately make the entire program run more smoothly and efficiently, benefiting both us and the client.

6.2.2 Understand the people behind their roles

Understanding each stakeholder's role and influence within the organization is essential, but even more important is taking the time to know the person behind the role. Building rapport is key, and often, it's the informal moments—like water cooler chats or coffee conversations—that help establish trust. This is one of the most important activities you'll want to invest in during the early stages of a transformation program.

Diagram 46: Understand People behind their Roles

Spending time upfront to build these relationships will greatly benefit both sides, as it helps leaders navigate the program more effectively and efficiently. It's also useful to map these stakeholders to the sign-offs and approvals they'll be responsible for throughout the program. Having a mix of formal and informal discussions to socialize these ideas can go a long way in fostering trust and building a solid, long-term relationship.

Caselet 9

One of my clients was quite aggressive in the early weeks of the engagement. During a few informal meetings, I took the opportunity to understand her deeper motivations and learned that her aspiration was to get promoted after the successful completion of the transformation. Once I uncovered her goal, I reassured her that we would deliver our solution on time and rallied my team to align with this shared objective. As she witnessed our commitment to her success, her attitude shifted—she became incredibly supportive and appreciative during reviews. This camaraderie not only eased the engagement but also helped solidify a long-term relationship with the client that lasted for three years.

6.2.3 Baseline efforts during discovery to avoid future surprises

Diagram 47: Baseline Efforts

I can't stress enough the importance of baselining scope and effort at the beginning of any large transformation program, especially during the discovery phase. The sales cycle is typically short, and the pursuit team only engages with a limited number of stakeholders. As a result, the scope is captured at a high level based on the limited time and context available.

During discovery, however, you'll interact with many more stakeholders, each bringing different perspectives and insights.

The partner team must approach this phase with empathy, carefully capturing all the new information to properly baseline the scope. This process is both an art and a science. It's essential to establish clear guardrails - such as integration touchpoints, assumptions, and dependencies—and use these to refine the initial estimates.

As you collect this new, detailed information, compare it against what your team understood during the sales process. Naturally, there will be some discrepancies, which is the entire point of the discovery exercise. Map these new insights to the bigger picture and assess their impact on your estimates. This will guide your team in creating a more accurate baseline project plan for the next phase.

If there are any significant differences, flag them early to leadership, backed with data points to support your case, and work toward a new shared understanding. Delaying this baselining process introduces unnecessary risks to the program, which could escalate as execution progresses.

6.2.4 Collaborative Workshops Drive Co-creation

Diagram 48: Collaborative Workshops than Meetings

Workshops not only enhance efficiency but also create a culture of collaboration and trust. By setting up the right collaboration environment from the start, you minimize delays often caused by fragmented communication across multiple meetings. Bringing everyone in the same room for problem-solving speeds up decision-making. More importantly, workshops encourage direct interaction, brainstorming, and shared ownership of solutions, building trust as everyone feels heard and part of the process.

Beyond tactical discussions, these workshops provide an ideal space for strategic alignment - whether it's understanding program objectives, identifying key metrics for success, or baselining those metrics. These are not tasks that can be effectively handled in a series of scattered meetings. A workshop allows for thorough discussion, perspective sharing, and co-creation, ensuring that all parties are aligned from the beginning.

Co-creation should be the default approach whenever possible, from user journeys and persona creation to wireframes and even the project plan itself. The most effective planning I've ever been part of was co-created with key client stakeholders in their office. By working together, we identified critical dependencies, mapped out user journeys, and addressed gaps before finalizing the plan. This collaborative process significantly increases the success rate, as it secures greater buy-in from both sides. Everyone agrees on the assumptions, and risks are mitigated collectively.

Ultimately, workshops are essential not only for efficient decision-making but also for fostering co-creation. They help teams to collaboratively craft solutions, identify risks early, and build a foundation of trust - all of which are essential ingredients for a successful transformation program.

Heat Map Based Risk Register

Risk ID	Risks	Raised date	Likelihood of occurrence	Impact if this occurs	Overall severity (based on likelihood and impact)	Risk owner
1	Complex API integrations (Appx 10)	6-Sep	High	High	High	Integration lead
2	Non availability of security testing tool	6-Sep	Medium	High	High	Infosec lead
3	Non availability of pre-prod environment for load testing	6-Sep	Low	Low	Low	Infra lead
4	Sign-off delays	15-Sep	Medium	Medium	Medium	PM
5	Unplanned sick leave of key people in the program	20-Sep	Low	Medium	Low	PM
6	Unavailability of UAT people	25-Sep	Medium	High	High	UAT lead

Diagram 49: Heatmap based Risk Register

6.2.5 Risk Management is a Program Habit:

Risk management should be ingrained as a habit, not just a virtue. The Project Manager (usually from the partner team or the team with the largest scope) must establish a risk register from day one. It's important to organize a workshop with key stakeholders to identify and document risks as early as possible. Regularly reviewing and prioritizing these risks - ideally on a weekly basis - should be a standard part of program management.

There are various ways to make risks visible. A heatmap-based risk register is both simple and effective, while a Risk Priority Number (RPN) register offers a more objective approach. By aligning on the severity, likelihood, and detection of each risk, you can prioritize using the RPN score.

It's also crucial to assign clear ownership for each risk and ensure a mitigation plan is in place. If mitigation actions remain unresolved for too long, the Project Manager should escalate to senior leaders to help address and mitigate those risks.

6.2.6 Motivated Teams Fuel Transformation

Keeping your team motivated is often the biggest challenge in an intense transformation program. It's essential to design the program in a way that excites people, encourages them to bring their best efforts, and offers clear opportunities for growth. During staffing conversations, it's crucial to ask probing questions to understand what each individual is hoping to gain from the program (What's In It For Me - WIFME).

Onboarding should include steps to capture each person's strengths, areas for growth, and career aspirations. Where possible, assign a mentor or performance partner who can provide guidance and align their development within the program. Establishing up a regular feedback loop from the beginning ensures team members feel supported, and any issues can be addressed early.

RPN Based Risk Register

Risk ID	Risks	Raised date	Severity of risk, if occurs (1-10)	Likelihood of Occurrence if occurs (1-10)	Difficulty of the risk for being detected (1-10)	RPN [Risk Priority Number] (Severity x Occurrence x Detection)	Risk owner
1	Complex API integrations (Appx 10)	6-Sep	10	8	8	640	Integration lead
2	Non availability of security testing tool	6-Sep	9	4	3	108	Infosec lead
3	Non availability of pre-prod environment for load testing	6-Sep	9	4	3	108	Infra lead
4	Sign-off delays	15-Sep					PM
5	Unplanned sick leave of key people in the program	20-Sep	8	5	7	280	PM
6	Unavailability of UAT people	25-Sep	8	5	3	120	UAT lead

Diagram 50: RPN based Risk Register

Name	Current Role	Responsibilities in the Program	Strengths	Growth Areas	Aspirational role	Growth plan
Amit Chawla	Business Analyst	Creation of Product backlog, story grooming, value-based prioritisation	Good domain understanding, tech depth, string in story analysis, driving estimation	Articulation skills, negotiation skills	Product Manager	Provide coaching for next 6 months, review in 6 months to check readiness for Proma role in the same program
Parth M	Full stack developer	Full stack development (75% individual contribution), 25% mentoring 3-4 Devs in the team	Great tech skills across front and back-end tech stack, Tech analysis and approachable to team member	Yields to high pressure environment, Not good in delegation	Data Engineer	Coaching on job, nomination for DE bootcamp in 6 months' time
Neha	Quality engineer	Test planning, testcase creations, testing and UAT support to client	Effective analysis, exploratory testing, good client communication	Collaboration, planning and structuring ambiguity	On-shore QA Lead	Mentoring by PM, look out for onshore opportunity in a year's time

Diagram 51: People Growth Tracker - An Illustrative example

Program leaders play a vital role in ensuring these personal goals are met. There should be a concerted effort to create opportunities within the program that align with individual aspirations, making it a win for the people involved, a win for the client leadership who will benefit from a highly motivated team, and a win for the partner leadership who will see better performance and results. It's this win-win-win approach that leads to long-term success for everyone involved.

6.2.7 Empower team with lean governance

Why do people resist governance? It's often because autonomous teams and governance seem at odds. On one hand, we talk about empowering teams to make decisions; on the other, governance is seen as putting controls on that autonomy. This dichotomy creates tension, but there's a way to balance both without leaning into micromanagement.

A lightweight governance structure can guide a program without stifling creativity. Begin by brainstorming with the team to define what governance should look like for the program. Empower the team to handle day-to-day decision-making while establishing clear thresholds for when they need to escalate issues—such as when critical milestones are at risk or budget variance exceeds a set limit. This creates a culture of "pull," where the team seeks leadership support when needed, rather than feeling pushed by constant oversight.

For governance meetings, it's crucial to keep the group small, ideally with only those responsible for key decisions. More than 6-7 people can make the meetings inefficient. Use simple tools like Trello, Excel, or Google Sheets to track decisions and publish them centrally, ensuring transparency without adding unnecessary layers of control. This approach fosters autonomy while keeping the program on track.

D ID	Decision Description	Why this Decision	Decision Impact	Decision Team	Decision Date
1	Dev approach to include mobile apps and web responsive portal to support native features for better stickiness	Earlier decision for web/mobile responsive portal is being challenged by Product Owner due to anticipated poor adoption	Cost of Development is expected to go up. Dev Partner to provide additional cost to support this.	CTO, Product Owner	10-Sep
2	UAT support of 3 weeks to be provided for each production builc	Earlier decision of 1 week UAT is not sufficient despite continuous QA along with dev cycles due to multiple edge case scenarios.	MVP Launch date will get impacted duo extended UAT for each production release	Product Owner, UAT Lead, Engineering Manager, Partner Project Manager	15-Sep
3	Client team to get co-located to partner's team location for co-creation of UX designs	Remote reviews of UX deliverables (wires and VDs) are taking longer and impacting project timelines	Client team travel cost to be included as CAPEX	Business Sponsor, Client PM, Partner PM	15-Sep

Diagram 52: Light Weight Decison Log: An Illustrative example

6.3 Potential role of AI and GenAI in the complex execution?

As technology rapidly evolves, the execution of complex transformation programs is set on the verge of a significant shift, driven by the integration of AI and Generative AI (GenAI). These advanced technologies are poised to revolutionize how organizations approach and manage large-scale projects, bringing about changes in everything from decision-making processes to the productivity of developers.

AI and GenAI are already making waves in various industries, and their impact on complex transformation programs may be significant. These technologies have the potential to enhance project execution by improving decision-making, optimizing resource allocation, and enabling more accurate predictions of project outcomes. But the real game-changer lies in how AI and GenAI can transform the way teams work, especially when it comes to software development.

6.3.1 Enhanced Decision-Making and Risk Management

One of the most critical aspects of executing complex transformation programs is the ability to make informed decisions quickly and effectively. AI can process vast amounts of data in real-time, providing insights that help project managers and stakeholders to make better decisions. This includes figuring out important hypotheses so that the team can do proof of concepts and make go/no-go decisions on them. This may also include identifying potential risks, predicting project delays, and optimizing resource allocation. Through AI-driven analytics, teams can also uncover patterns that may not be immediately apparent, allowing for more proactive risk management. For example, AI can analyze historical data from previous projects to predict the likelihood of certain risks occurring in a current project. This allows teams to take preventive measures before issues arise, reducing the chances of project delays and cost overruns. Additionally, AI can help in scenario planning by simulating different project paths and their potential outcomes, enabling teams to choose the most efficient and effective route.

Organizations with varying levels of data availability and platform maturity will experience different impacts from AI and GenAI. Those with lower data maturity will need to prioritize data collection and focus on creating a robust data value chain before harnessing the power of AI and Machine Learning (ML) and in contrast, organizations with higher maturity are more likely to apply AI to identify patterns and apply machine learning algorithms to enhance decision-making.

6.3.2 Automating Routine Tasks and Enhancing Developer Productivity

One of the most immediate benefits of AI and GenAI in complex transformation programs is the automation of routine tasks. This includes code generation, test case generation, automation of testing, and even aspects of project management.

The advent of Generative AI tools, such as GitHub Copilot, has revolutionized the productivity landscape for developers, drastically altering the pace and efficiency of software development. These tools enable developers to write code faster, with fewer errors, and with more creativity. By offering real-time code suggestions, automated bug detection, and even the ability to generate entire code snippets based on natural language prompts, GenAI tools reduce the cognitive load on developers, enabling them to focus on higher-level problem-solving. The productivity gains associated with using AI-driven tools may be substantial. Developers can focus more on creative problem-solving and innovation rather than getting bogged down in mundane tasks. This increase in productivity may lead to faster project delivery times and potentially lower costs.

6.3.3 Impact on Project Estimations and Speed

With AI and GenAI tools streamlining the development process, the way project estimates are made will also change. Traditionally, estimations have relied on historical data, expert judgment, and some degree of guesswork. However, AI can analyze large datasets to provide more accurate estimations, taking into account various factors such as team productivity, complexity of tasks, and potential risks.

For instance, AI can predict how long it will take to complete a specific task by analyzing how similar tasks have been handled in the past. It can also consider the productivity levels of individual team members incorporating the use of AI-driven tools like Copilot. This can lead to more realistic timelines and budgets, reducing the likelihood of project delays and cost overruns.

With AI handling routine tasks and providing real-time insights, teams can move faster and with more confidence. This can be particularly beneficial in agile environments where rapid iteration and continuous delivery are key.

6.3.4 Facilitating Collaboration and Communication

Effective collaboration and communication are essential for the success of any transformation program, especially when dealing with complex, multi-faceted projects. AI and GenAI might play a pivotal role in enhancing these aspects by providing tools that facilitate better communication, automate reporting, and ensure that everyone is on the same page.

For example, AI-driven project management tools can automatically generate progress reports, track key performance indicators, and even send reminders for upcoming deadlines. This reduces the administrative burden on team members and ensures that stakeholders are always informed about the project's status. Additionally, AI can help bridge communication gaps by providing real-time translation and transcription services, making it easier for global teams to collaborate effectively.

6.3.5 Future-Ready Project Management

As AI and GenAI continue to evolve, their role in project management will become even more significant. Future project managers will need to be well-versed in these technologies to fully leverage their potential. This includes understanding how to interpret AI-driven insights, how to integrate AI tools into existing workflows, and how to manage the ethical implications of using AI in decision-making.

In the future, we can expect AI to take on an even more proactive role in project management. For example, AI could autonomously monitor project progress, identify potential issues before they arise, and suggest solutions in real-time. This would allow project managers to focus more on strategic decision-making rather than day-to-day operations.

6.3.6 The Role of AI in Managing Complexity

Complex transformation programs often involve multiple teams, technologies, and stakeholders. Managing this complexity can be challenging, but AI has the potential to make it more manageable. AI can help teams navigate the complexities of large-scale projects by providing a holistic view of the entire program, highlighting dependencies, and identifying potential bottlenecks.

For example, AI can analyze the interdependencies between different tasks and suggest ways to optimize the critical path. It can also monitor the progress of individual tasks and alert the team if any task is falling behind schedule. This allows teams to address issues before they escalate and ensures that the project stays on track.

Moreover, AI can assist in managing the complexity of integrating new technologies into existing systems. By simulating different integration scenarios, AI can help teams identify potential issues and develop solutions before implementation. This reduces the risk of disruptions during the integration process and ensures a smoother transition.

To sum it up, the integration of AI and GenAI into the execution of complex transformation programs is not just a possibility; it is an inevitability. These technologies are already demonstrating their potential to enhance productivity, improve decision-making, and manage complexity. As they continue to evolve, their impact will only grow, fundamentally changing how large-scale projects are executed.

For developers, project managers, and stakeholders alike, embracing AI and GenAI will be key to staying competitive in the rapidly changing technological landscape. The future of complex transformation programs is here, and it is being shaped by the transformative power of artificial intelligence.

Chapter 7

The Art and Science of Change Management

7.0 It's All About Change Management!

So far, we've explored how technological evolution has enabled businesses to leverage digital transformation to grow and scale. However, choosing the right technology partner is a complex task, as it involves multiple decision-makers and influencers, as mentioned in Chapter 5.2.2. Once technology partners are chosen, the real challenge for businesses begins: adapting to the changes introduced by transformation initiatives.

Let me clarify the two types of "Change" we're discussing in our context:

1. **Change Requests (CR)** - These refer to changes in scope regularly identified by program managers working on the digital product being developed. Such changes follow a formal change request management process, which is covered in detail in Chapter 6.1.4, under the 4th bullet point.
2. **Organizational Changes Driven by Transformation Initiatives** – Large digital transformation programs involve more than merely selecting and implementing the best technology solutions. They require a deep understanding of existing business processes, identifying challenges, and often re-engineering workflows. This might mean automating repetitive tasks, eliminating manual steps, and introducing digital solutions powered by APIs within a broader ecosystem.

For example, in automating the lending process, you wouldn't just automate existing steps. Instead, it should reimagine the process by leveraging digital possibilities, such as using APIs that can integrate with banking systems to bring bank statements and credit bureaus to assess creditworthiness. Whether it's reimagining the process or automating some steps powered by the digital ecosystem, expect some changes in the way the team is currently engaged. These changes often push people to adopt new ways of working, which can be difficult.

Managing these organization-wide changes requires a proactive, systematic approach. Before diving into how to manage these changes, let's first explore why people tend to resist these **'Changes'** in the first place

7.1 Why Do We Resist Change?

Whether it's a digital transformation journey, a reorganization of business verticals within an enterprise, or addressing a major scope change in a digital transformation program, they all create a **certain level of resistance** in our brains. Perhaps the real question we should be asking ourselves is:

"Why does every change in our lives elicit resistance?"

What do Human behavior studies suggest?

Let's explore the understanding of resistance to change through the lens of Louise D. Bringselius' research. In his 2012 thesis at Lund University, Sweden, Bringselius delves into the phenomenon of "resistance" and presents four key interpretations *(Bringselius, 2010)*:

Louise D. Bringselius explains how people resist change in various situations and how difficult it might be to change their minds.

Changeability of resistance: This means how easy or hard it is to get someone to change their mind or behavior.

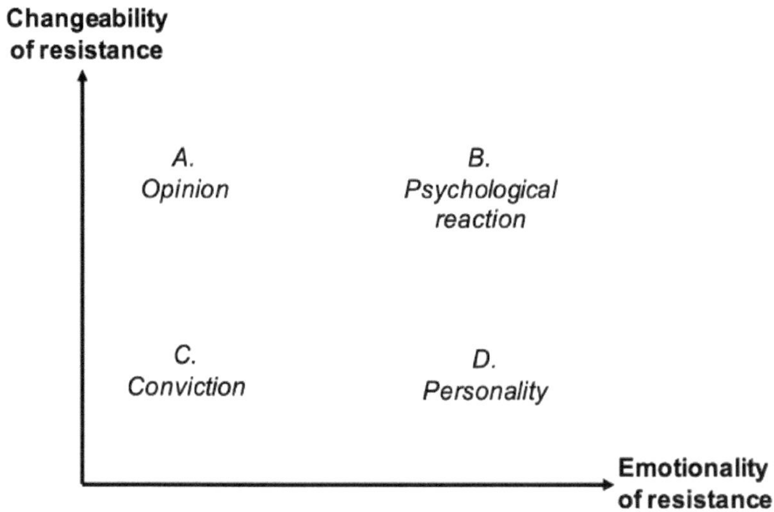

Diagram 53: Lousie framework of Resistance

Emotionality of resistance: This shows how much emotion is involved in the resistance. The more emotional someone is about their resistance, the harder it might be to change their mind.

The four areas of the chart break down like this:

A. **Opinion (High changeability, low emotionality):** These are people who have a viewpoint or preference but aren't very emotionally attached to it. They're pretty easy to persuade if you give them a good reason.

B. **Psychological reaction (High changeability, high emotionality)**: These people are very emotional about their resistance, but with the right approach, they can be convinced to change. You might need to address their feelings first before they'll listen to reason.

C. **Conviction (Low changeability, low emotionality):** These people have strong beliefs that are hard to change, but they're not overly emotional about it. Changing their minds will be tough because their resistance is based on firm principles.

D. **Personality (Low changeability, high emotionality):** This is the most challenging group. They are deeply emotional and hold strong beliefs, making them the hardest to persuade or change.

Research also suggests that resistance should not be understood as negative emotions all the time. Sometimes resistance can be seen as evidence of loyalty and if properly used, can enhance the prospects for successful implementation.

In Louise's interpretation model, he suggests different ways to overcome resistance. First, resistance can be reduced through proper dialogue, allowing for negotiation and plan adjustments (**Interpretation A**). Second, workshops or in-depth discussions may help people accept the changes (**Interpretation B**). For those guided by strong morals and ethics, purpose-driven conversations can resolve conflicts and improve decision-making (**Interpretation C**). Lastly, for highly emotional individuals resistant to change, rotating them may be a better solution (**Interpretation D**).

While the above research explains resistance towards change from human behavior studies, what does neuroscience suggest on this "change phenomenon"?

What do Neuroscience studies show?

We, the human race, are an evolved species and have two regions of the brain. Upper brain (prefrontal cortex) and lower brain (amygdala).

The amygdala is the part of the brain focused on survival, keeping us safe from uncertainty. It helps us navigate familiar situations and operate on autopilot. It also triggers immediate reactions like fear or aggression when faced with change, leading to resistance.

In contrast to the amygdala, the prefrontal cortex (PFC) is responsible for reasoning and decision-making. It enables us to think rationally, and become mature over time. While our brains learn from experience, they also get used to doing things a certain way. When faced with a new approach (a "change"), our amygdala often resists unless we engage the PFC. So, when and how can we engage our PFC?

We do this when we believe that the change is good, which requires a shift in mindset.

"But is change good?"

How does Cognitive research explain this?

Cognitive science research highlights that change is beneficial for the brain. It stimulates neurons, builds new neural pathways, and even helps delay the effects of aging. When we experience new situations or adapt to changes, our brain gets stronger and more flexible, improving cognitive function and mental health.

What is the systemic way of dealing with change?

On an organizational level, embracing change is equally important. It fosters innovation, drives progress, and helps businesses stay competitive in a rapidly evolving market. However, it's essential to approach change as a systemic process. This means understanding that change isn't just about introducing new tools or methods, it's about reshaping the way teams work, think, and collaborate. When managed well, change creates growth opportunities, allowing organizations to develop new capabilities, address challenges, and achieve long-term success.

Let's look at a systemic framework to deal with the **'Change'**.

7.2 Framework to deal with the 'Change'

To better understand and manage resistance to change in an organization, we can turn to Gleicher's formula, later refined by Dannemiller and others, which outlines how dissatisfaction, vision, first steps, and support can help leaders overcome resistance to change *(Dannemiller & Jacobs, 1992)*. This formula, expressed as:

D x V x F x S > Resistance (R)

Illustrates that if these factors (Dissatisfaction, Vision, First steps, and Support) are strong enough, they will collectively outweigh the natural resistance that people feel toward change.

Let's explore each element in detail and how leaders can utilize them to manage and implement change effectively.

1. Dissatisfaction (D)

The first key element in overcoming resistance is dissatisfaction. Dissatisfaction refers to the current pain points, frustrations, or inefficiencies in the system or organization that people experience daily. Without a sense of dissatisfaction, people are generally content to maintain the status quo. Change often requires an energy or motivation to move away from the present situation, and dissatisfaction provides this initial push.

As a leader, your role here is to bring this dissatisfaction to the forefront. It's crucial to openly communicate why the current state is no longer sustainable. Whether it's inefficiencies in the process, declining customer satisfaction, falling behind competitors, or an outdated technology platform, people need to clearly see what's not working. This dissatisfaction should be articulated in a way that resonates with the team's daily experience. When individuals understand that staying where they are could lead to negative consequences for the business, it helps reduce their reluctance to embrace change.

However, it's important to strike a balance. Overemphasizing dissatisfaction can lead to fear or demoralization. Instead, the goal is to highlight dissatisfaction just enough to build a sense of urgency, motivating the team to take action, while leaving space for optimism and forward movement.

2. Vision (V)

Once the dissatisfaction with the current state has been acknowledged, the next step is to present a **compelling vision of the future**. This vision must effectively answer the question: What does the future look like once the change is successfully implemented? People are more likely to embrace change when they have a clear understanding of what they're working towards and what the end result will be.

A strong vision creates a sense of purpose, aligning everyone's efforts toward a common goal. It provides clarity and direction, helping team members understand that the discomfort of change will ultimately lead to positive outcomes. As a leader, it is your responsibility to paint a vivid picture of what success looks like. Will the company be more efficient, innovative, or profitable? Will employees have better tools, improved workflows, or more rewarding roles? The more concrete and relatable the vision is, the more buy-in you'll get from your team.

To ensure that the vision resonates, it should be communicated in a way that reflects the values and priorities of the team. For instance, if the team values efficiency, your vision should focus on how the change will make their work faster and more streamlined. If they value customer satisfaction, the vision should emphasize how the change will lead to better customer experiences. A well-crafted vision answers the "what's in it for me?" question for every stakeholder.

3. First Steps (F)

Even with a strong sense of dissatisfaction and a clear vision of the future, change can still feel overwhelming if it's not broken down into manageable steps. This is where the **third element**, **First Steps**, comes into play. First steps refer to the initial actions that need to be taken to start moving toward the desired outcome.

The key here is to simplify the process. When people see a clear path forward, they're less likely to feel overwhelmed by the scope of the change. It's important to outline specific, achievable actions that help the team make progress right away. These steps should be small enough that they don't feel daunting yet significant enough to generate momentum. This helps reduce the uncertainty that comes with change, making it easier for people to get on board.

As a leader, you can help guide the team through these initial steps by breaking down large goals into smaller, more attainable milestones. Celebrating small wins along the way to keep the team motivated and focused. This approach helps build confidence in the team's ability to manage change and demonstrates that progress is being made. It's essential to communicate that these initial actions are not just tasks but critical building blocks for achieving larger success down the road.

4. Support (S)

Finally, support is the fourth critical component for overcoming resistance to change. No change process can succeed without the **right level of support**. This support can take many forms, including resources, training, mentorship, guidance, and emotional encouragement. Support ensures that as people navigate through the challenges of change, they don't feel isolated or unsupported.

Leadership support is essential, but so is peer support. Teams need to feel that they're in this together and that their efforts are recognized and appreciated. As a leader, providing continuous feedback and reassurance can keep the momentum going. Offering learning opportunities, and resources to ease the transition, and being available to answer questions and concerns can significantly alleviate the anxiety that comes with change.

It's also important to establish a support system that goes beyond just management. Designating change ambassadors or champions within the team can be an effective strategy to build support. These individuals can act as role models and provide peer guidance, helping others navigate the change process more smoothly. Additionally, leaders should make it clear that mistakes are a natural part of the learning process, and that there is room for adjustment as the team moves forward.

Overcoming Resistance (R)

Resistance to change is a natural human response, and it's something every leader must address when leading a transformation. People may resist for various reasons - fear of the unknown, concern over their job security, or simply the discomfort of having to learn new skills or processes.

Gleicher's formula emphasizes that when dissatisfaction, vision, first steps, and support are strong enough, they will collectively outweigh this resistance.

D x V x F x S > Resistance (R)

This approach has been tested and proven successful in numerous organizational settings. By focusing on each of these elements, leaders can create an environment that not only encourages change but also reduces fear and provides the necessary tools needed to navigate the transformation effectively.

As a leader, it's our job to guide the team through this process.

First, make sure the dissatisfaction with the current situation is clear. People need to understand why staying where they are is no longer viable.

Then, inspire them with a compelling vision of what the future holds after the change.

Provide them with clear first steps to help them move forward without feeling overwhelmed.

Finally, ensure that they have the right level of support throughout the journey.

When all these elements - dissatisfaction, vision, first steps, and support - are aligned, the resistance to change becomes much easier to manage, and you're more likely to succeed in implementing meaningful and lasting changes.

7.3 How to Operationalise the Change?

Operationalizing change management is a key to making successful transformations in an organization. It's not just about introducing new systems or processes; it's about creating a strategy that meets the needs of the organization, its employees, and stakeholders. Here's a simple guide on strategies to effectively put change management into action, ensuring a smooth and meaningful transformation.

7.3.1 Craft Key Changes with Baseline Metrics and Desired Goals

7.3.2 Communicate Progress with Objective Dashboards

7.3.2 Collect Continuous Feedback and Pivoting When Needed

7.3.4 Foster Open, Bi-Directional Communication

7.3.5 Appoint and Empower Change Ambassadors

7.3.6 Offer Learning Opportunities to Enhance Cognitive Flexibility

7.3.7 Encourage Community-Driven Creative Platforms

7.3.1 Craft key changes with Baseline Metrics and Desired Goals

To begin with, it's essential to lay a solid foundation by identifying and crafting the key changes required for the transformation. This involves a thorough analysis of the current state of the organization and the specific areas where change is necessary.

Start by conducting a needs assessment to pinpoint the areas that require transformation. Engage with various stakeholders, including employees, customers, and leadership, to understand their perspectives and gather insights into what changes are necessary. This process might involve analyzing existing workflows, technology stacks, customer feedback, and competitive benchmarks.

Once the key changes are identified, establish baseline metrics to understand the current performance levels. These metrics should be quantitative and specific, such as productivity rates, customer satisfaction scores, or financial performance indicators. Baseline metrics provide a clear understanding of where the organization stands before the implementation of changes, which is crucial for measuring progress and success.

Set clear, measurable goals aligned with the desired outcomes of the transformation. These goals should be SMART (Specific, Measurable, Achievable, Relevant, Time-bound) to ensure clarity and focus. For instance, if the goal is to improve customer satisfaction, specify the target satisfaction score, the timeline for achieving it, and the steps required to reach this target.

Communicate the goals and expectations to all stakeholders involved. This helps in managing expectations and ensuring everyone is on the same page regarding what the transformation aims to achieve. Establishing these expectations early on also aids in securing buy-in and support from key stakeholders.

7.3.2 Communicate Progress with Objective Dashboards

Effective communication is crucial in managing change. Objective dashboards are a powerful tool for tracking and communicating progress.

Create dashboards that visually represent progress toward the established goals. These dashboards should be user-friendly, with clear visual indicators such as charts, graphs, and progress bars. They should provide real-time data and be easily accessible to all stakeholders.

Regularly update the dashboards to reflect the latest data and progress. Transparency is key to maintaining trust and keeping stakeholders informed about the status of the transformation. This transparency helps in identifying any issues early on and allows for timely interventions.

Use the data from the dashboards to make informed decisions. Regularly review the progress and adjust strategies as needed based on the insights gained. Data-driven decision-making ensures that actions are aligned with the goals and that the transformation remains on track.

7.3.3 Collect Continuous Feedback and Pivoting When Needed

Feedback is a vital component of managing change. It provides valuable insights into how the transformation is being received and highlights areas that may require adjustment.

Implement various feedback mechanisms such as surveys, focus groups, and suggestion boxes. Engage with employees at all levels to gather their input and perspectives. This feedback can reveal challenges, concerns, and areas where the change may not be meeting expectations.

Regularly analyze the feedback collected to identify common themes and trends. Look for patterns that indicate areas of resistance or dissatisfaction. Use this analysis to make informed adjustments to the change strategy and address any issues that arise.

Adopt an agile approach to change management. Be prepared to pivot and make adjustments based on the feedback received. This flexibility helps in maintaining the relevance and effectiveness of the transformation efforts.

7.3.4 Foster Open, Bi-Directional Communication

Effective communication is not a one-way street; it involves ongoing dialogue between the leaders and the employees.

Establish open communication channels such as interactive town halls, forums, or digital platforms where employees can ask questions, express concerns, and share ideas. These channels should encourage open dialogue and provide a space for employees to voice out their thoughts.

Host regular Q&A sessions with leaders to address any concerns or questions that the employees may have. These sessions should be interactive, allowing for real-time responses and discussions. Transparency in these sessions helps build trust and confidence in the change process.

Fostering trust through bi-directional communication involves actively listening to employees and addressing their concerns. Ensure that feedback is taken seriously and acted upon, demonstrating that leadership values employee input and is committed to making necessary changes.

7.3.5 Appoint and Empower Change Ambassadors

Change ambassadors play a crucial role in advocating for the transformation and helping to drive its success.

Select change ambassadors from various departments and levels within the organization. These individuals should be respected, influential, and enthusiastic about the change. They will act as advocates, assisting their peers and promoting the benefits of the transformation.

Acknowledge and reward the efforts of change ambassadors who actively contribute to the transformation. Recognition can come in various forms, such as public praise, career development opportunities, etc. This recognition reinforces positive behaviors and encourages others to support the change process.

7.3.6 Offer Learning Opportunities to Enhance Cognitive Flexibility

Learning opportunities are crucial for preparing employees for the challenges of transformation and fostering a growth mindset.

Offer training programs that align with the goals of the transformation. This may include technical training, leadership development, and soft skills workshops. Ensure that the training is relevant and tailored to the needs of different employee groups.

Promote a culture of continuous learning by providing ongoing development opportunities. Encourage employees to pursue further education, attend industry conferences, or participate in professional development activities.

Support cognitive flexibility by encouraging employees to explore new ideas and approaches. Provide opportunities for creative problem-solving and innovative thinking, which can help employees adapt to change more effectively.

7.3.7 Encourage Community-Driven Creative Platforms

Creative platforms can play a significant role in fostering a positive and cohesive work environment.

Establish spaces where employees can engage in creative activities such as music, dance, theater, or art. These spaces provide a supportive environment for self-expression and team bonding.

There are organization which host events that encourage creative participation, such as talent shows, art exhibitions, or team-building activities. These events help reduce stress, build camaraderie, and create a sense of community within the organization.

Encourage team bonding through collaborative creative projects. These projects can help build stronger relationships among team members and foster a more supportive and adaptable work environment.

By integrating these strategies, we can create a holistic approach to change management that addresses various aspects of the transformation process. This comprehensive approach ensures that the organization remains agile, employees feel supported, and the transformation objectives are achieved with minimal resistance.

The Role of AI in driving change management

AI tools are becoming powerful choices in driving change management by making the process more efficient and data-driven. AI may help in analyzing employee sentiment, predicting resistance points, and providing insights to guide decision-making. GenAI can assist in creating personalized communication strategies, training materials, and FAQs tailored to different stakeholders, making the change process smoother and more engaging. While these technologies have the potential to support many aspects of change management, it's essential to remember they can't replace the human element. Building trust, fostering open communication, and addressing emotional responses are still critical. AI and GenAI can support the process, but successful change management ultimately requires a balance between technology and human understanding.

Chapter 8

Leadership Styles for Large-Scale Transformation

8.0 Leadership styles for a large transformation

Large transformation programs are inherently complex, involving numerous moving parts, competing priorities, and often conflicting interests. These programs require the coordination of diverse teams, each with different objectives and expertise, all working towards a common goal. Leaders at the helm of these programs face a continuous balancing act. They must navigate constraints like limited resources, time pressures, and the need to deliver tangible results. Trade-offs are inevitable, and leaders are often required to make difficult decisions that may not satisfy everyone but are necessary to keep the program on course. This demands not only a strong grasp of the program's technical and strategic aspects but also the ability to manage relationships, build consensus, and sustain the team's morale.

Caselet 11

"Five months into a large fixed-bid digital transformation program, our partner team faced an issue that stemmed from inaccurate estimates. As the engagement lead, along with the program's UX lead and tech lead, we found ourselves in a tough spot. We had to figure out how to explain the potential delay of 2-3 months to the client and seek buy-in from the senior leadership team.

After carefully discussing our options, we approached our business head to explain the situation. To our surprise, he listened intently for almost an hour and invited one of us to start brainstorming on the whiteboard. He remained calm and composed, challenging us to think creatively and find solutions that wouldn't impact the timeline.

When we struggled with our limited ideas, he began suggesting different scenarios. After 3-4 hours of workshopping, we had 4-5 alternative solutions. Within the next couple of days, we found a creative way forward. Instead of developing 18 separate templates for a complex AEM-driven website, we settled on using 6 unique templates with 85% reusable components to build almost 350 pages of varying complexity and functionality. This approach significantly reduced our timeline challenges, bringing us back on track to meet expectations.

While we were stuck with our problem, our business head operated with a fluid mindset and saw an opportunity for innovation. He didn't impose a solution on us but instead shifted his leadership style as needed; acting as a coach, a mentor, and finally a team member to help brainstorm alongside us. By the time we were close to solving the issue, his adaptable leadership made all the difference.

In our debrief, we were full of praise for his approach and leadership style."

Whether you're a frontline leader, such as a Program Business Analyst (BA), Technical Lead (TL), or Program Manager of a complex transformation program, constantly navigating uncertainty and ambiguity, or you're part of the senior leadership team providing executive oversight to such a critical initiative, you'll likely relate to some of the leadership traits outlined below. You may have already employed these traits to tackle challenges, or you might see an opportunity to further hone them to better steer your team. Let's dive into some of these essential leadership traits.

8.1 Leadership traits for a complex transformation programs

8.1.1 Exhibiting Resilience, Tenacity, and Grit

What it means:

Resilience, tenacity, and grit refer to the ability to bounce back from setbacks, stay committed to long-term goals, and push through challenges with determination. It's about not giving up, even when things get tough, and maintaining a strong focus on achieving the desired outcome.

Why it's critical:

Large transformation programs are often unpredictable, with many obstacles and difficulties along the way. Leaders who exhibit resilience, tenacity, and grit can keep the program moving forward, even when faced with adversity. These qualities are crucial for maintaining momentum and ensuring that the team doesn't lose motivation during tough times.

How it helps the team:

When leaders demonstrate resilience, tenacity, and grit, it inspires the team to adopt a similar attitude. It creates a positive example of perseverance, encouraging team members to stay focused, while working through challenges, and remain committed to the program's success. This leadership approach fosters a strong, united team that is better equipped to handle the pressures and complexities of the transformation process.

8.1.2 Leveraging Trade-offs

What it means:

Working with trade-offs involves making decisions where you have to choose between different options, each with its own set of pros and cons. It's about recognizing that you can't have everything, so you must prioritize what's most important to achieve the program's goals, even if it means compromising on other aspects.

Why it's critical:

In large transformation programs, resources like time, budget, and manpower are often limited. Leaders must make tough choices about where to allocate these resources. Understanding trade-offs is essential because it ensures that the most critical aspects of the program receive the attention and resources they need, while less crucial elements are managed with available constraints.

How it helps the team:

When leaders effectively manage trade-offs, they provide clarity and direction for the team. This helps the team stay focused on what truly matters and avoid getting bogged down by less important tasks. It also reduces stress by setting realistic expectations, allowing the team to work more efficiently with a clear understanding of priorities.

8.1.3 Cultivating growth culture

What it means:

Cultivating a growth culture involves creating an environment where continuous learning, improvement, and innovation are encouraged. It's about fostering a mindset where team members feel safe to experiment, learn from mistakes, and develop new skills, all while striving to reach their full potential.

Why it's critical:

In a large transformation program, the landscape is constantly changing, and new challenges emerge regularly. A growth culture equips the team with the adaptability and creativity needed to navigate these changes. It encourages them to think outside the box, embrace new ideas, and continuously improve their performance, which is vital for the program's success.

How it helps the team:

When leaders cultivate a growth culture, they empower the team to take ownership of their development and contributions. This boosts morale and engagement, as team members feel valued and motivated to grow. It also enhances the team's ability to solve problems and innovate, leading to more effective and sustainable solutions throughout the program.

An essential aspect of cultivating a growth culture is recognizing the varying levels of maturity among individuals in the team. This awareness should guide whether you take on a mentor or coach role. Initially, you might need to offer guidance and support as a mentor, but this should be temporary. Transition into a coaching role, you give team members the space to discover their own solutions while acting as a sounding board.

8.1.4 Operating with Fluid Mindset

What it means:

Operating with a fluid mindset means being flexible and open to new ideas, even when you're working within fixed limits like budget, time, or resources. It's about thinking creatively and adapting to changes, despite the constraints you have to work with. A fluid mindset will help you manage the constantly changing scope of a project more effectively.

Why it's critical:

Even when you have strict constraints, it's important to stay flexible in your thinking. The dichotomy here lies in finding ways to adapt while staying within the program constraints. A fluid mindset helps you deal with constraints without getting stuck, allowing you to come up with new solutions and adjust as needed.

It reduces the stress of having to win every argument or debate. By allowing you to let go of some issues and prioritize others, it creates a buffer that helps you focus on what truly matters. This approach enables you to build long-term relationships and focus on overall goals rather than getting bogged down by daily transactions and minor issues.

How it helps the team:

When leaders show a fluid mindset, they inspire their team to think creatively and adapt to challenges. This approach helps the team see constraints as opportunities for innovation, rather than obstacles. It leads to more effective problem-solving and keeps the team motivated, even when working with limited resources.

8.1.5 Demonstrating Situational (leadership) Awareness

What it means:

Situational leadership means adjusting your leadership style based on the specific needs of the situation and the people you're working with. It's about being flexible and choosing the best approach for each scenario, whether it means being more hands-on or giving team members more independence.

Why it's critical:

Different situations and team members require different types of guidance. Situational leadership helps you respond effectively to varying circumstances, ensuring that you provide the right level of support and direction when it's needed. This adaptability is a key to managing diverse challenges and maintaining team effectiveness.

How it helps the team:

Example 1: If a team member is new to a task and needs detailed guidance, a situational leader will take a hands-on approach, providing step-by-step instructions and frequent check-ins. This support helps the team members learn quickly and build confidence.

Example 2: When the team is working on a well-understood project and is high on motivation, the leader may adopt a more delegating style, giving team members the freedom to make decisions and take ownership. This approach fosters autonomy and encourages innovative solutions.

Example 3: During a crisis or when facing unexpected challenges, a situational leader may become more directive, setting clear priorities and providing specific instructions to quickly address the issues. This helps the team stay focused and effective under pressure.

8.2 How to Develop these Leadership Traits

Growing your people with these leadership traits is challenging for any organization, but it is an essential and intentional effort that requires a deliberate and structured approach. Here's how some organizations have successfully cultivated these leadership qualities:

8.2.1 Building Resilience, Tenacity, and Grit

Give your people challenging projects that push their limits and require them to overcome obstacles. This helps them develop resilience and tenacity as they face and manage difficulties and foster an environment where people are encouraged to tackle problems head-on and find solutions, rather than avoiding them.

Provide mentorship and coaching to help your program leaders navigate challenges and build their confidence. Regular feedback helps them learn from experiences and improves their persistence. Most importantly recognize and reward those who show determination and grit in their roles. This reinforces the value of these traits and motivates others.

Encourage a culture where setbacks are viewed as learning opportunities rather than failures. Help people analyze what went wrong and how to improve.

8.2.2 Developing Skills in Managing Trade-Offs

Work with your L&D team to create a role-play based training focused on decision-making and trade-off management. This training may cover techniques for evaluating competing priorities, understanding constraints, and making balanced decisions. It helps program leaders develop the ability to assess trade-offs and choose the most effective course of action. Utilize simulation exercises that present people with common trade-off situations. These exercises allow people to practice evaluating and balancing trade-offs in a controlled environment, improving their decision-making skills and understanding of the implications of various choices.

Create some smaller work stream that requires people to make decisions involving trade-offs in the same or different initiative. This real-world experience helps them understand the impact of their decisions on various aspects of the initiatives and develop a balanced approach to managing competing demands. Pair new budding leaders with experienced mentors who can provide guidance on managing trade-offs. Mentors can share their experiences and offer insights into effective strategies for making balanced decisions.

After key decisions involving trade-offs, conduct debriefing sessions to analyze the outcomes and reflect on the decision-making process. This practice helps people learn from their experiences. Create more forums like this to encourage social learnings.

8.2.3 Cultivating a Growth Mindset

Offer regular training sessions, workshops, and learning resources that help potential leaders acquire new skills and knowledge. Encourage them to seek out learning opportunities proactively. Encourage them to experiment with new approaches and ideas. Support them in taking calculated risks and learning from the outcomes.

Implement regular feedback sessions where people receive constructive criticism and guidance. This helps them understand areas for improvement and motivates them to grow. Create opportunities for your team to learn from each other through peer reviews and collaborative projects.

Help team members set personal and professional development goals that challenge them to grow. Provide resources and support to help them achieve these goals.

8.2.4 Adopting a Fluid Mindset

Implement agile practices that require people to adapt quickly to changes and be flexible in their approach. This helps them develop a fluid mindset in dynamic environments. Demonstrate a fluid mindset yourself as a leader. Show how to adapt to changes and handle constraints creatively, setting an example for others to follow.

Give your team the autonomy to make decisions and solve problems on their own with some cover for critical items. This encourages them to think creatively and adapt their strategies as needed. Create a culture where people feel confident in trying new approaches and adapting to new circumstances as they hone their new leadership styles.

8.2.5 Enhancing Situational Leadership

Ask your team to sign-up for training that covers various leadership styles and techniques. Help them understand when and how to apply different approaches based on the situation and their team's needs. Use role-playing and simulation exercises to practice situational leadership. This allows your team to experience and respond to different scenarios in a controlled environment.

Implement job rotations or cross-functional projects that expose people to different roles and challenges. This helps them develop the ability to adapt their leadership style to various situations. Pair budding leaders with mentors who have experience in situational leadership. Some organizations implement shadowing programs where emerging leaders observe experienced leaders in real-world projects. Both shadowing and reverse shadowing approaches can provide valuable support and a safety net for first-time leaders.

Use self-assessment tools to help people evaluate their leadership styles and effectiveness. Encourage reflection on their experiences and how they handle various situations. Conduct regular debriefing sessions where people can discuss their experiences and receive feedback on their situational leadership skills.

The role of AI in developing leadership traits

AI is increasingly becoming a practical tool for leaders looking to assess, develop and refine their leadership traits. There are many leadership assessment tools that are using AI power to assess people's leadership themes and can help leaders gain insights into their behaviors, team dynamics, and decision-making patterns. For example, AI-driven feedback tools may analyze communication styles and emotional intelligence, offering actionable suggestions for improvement. This may help leaders better understand how their actions affect team morale and productivity.

AI-powered coaching systems are also becoming popular, providing leaders with real-time advice and support. These systems can simulate different leadership challenges, allowing leaders to practice decision-making, conflict resolution, and strategic thinking in a risk-free environment. This hands-on approach helps build confidence and adaptability.

Moreover, AI can monitor team sentiment and performance by analyzing patterns from various data sources like employee feedback, project timelines, and productivity metrics. This early detection of potential issues may enable leaders to act proactively, improving team dynamics and project outcomes.

However, while AI can offer significant benefits, it doesn't replace the human touch. Key leadership traits such as empathy, emotional intelligence, and relationship-building remain irreplaceable. AI is a tool to augment leadership, helping leaders become more aware of their strengths and blind spots, but effective leadership still depends on human judgment and emotional connection.

Bonus Chapter 9

Revenue Recognition in Transformation Programs

9.0 Revenue Recognition in Fixed Bid Engagements

This chapter aims to familiarize the Partner's team with the concepts of revenue recognition, in two most common scenarios. One is when the billing agreement between client and partner is based on the effort spent by the Partner's team with a pre-agreed hourly rate (**T&M engagements**). Two, when the billing agreement between client and partner is based on the pre-agreed deliverable by the partner's team on mutually agreed timelines (**Fixed Bid engagements**).

Before we dive into engagement specific nuances, let's understand the criteria of revenue recognition and the accounting principle behind this:

9.1 Criteria & Principles for Revenue Recognition

According to **GAAP** (Generally Accepted Accounting Principles), there are four criteria that need to be met for any revenue recognition.

1. The price of the product or services can be determined (Fixed price or Rate card).
2. Collection is probable (Agreed billing terms).
3. There is persuasive evidence of an arrangement (contract in place).

4. Delivery has occurred (User acceptance of product or service).

If we apply these principles in the context of software deliveries, here are four step methods that can help us recognize the revenue.

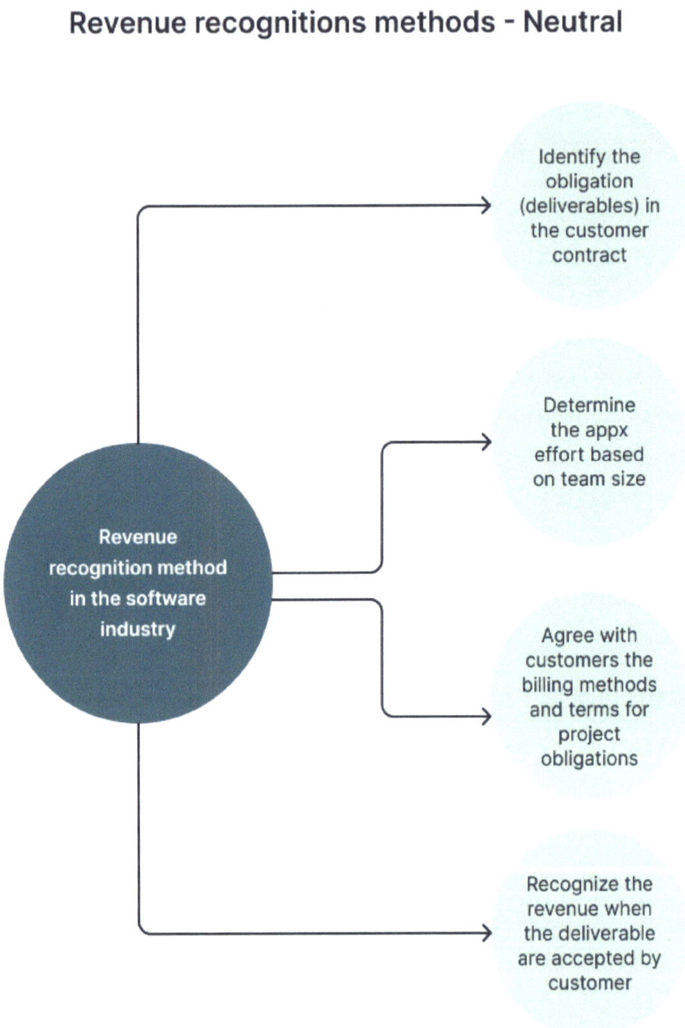

Diagram 54: Revenue Recognition Method in Software Services

Revenue recognition for T&M engagements:

In Time & Materials (T&M) engagements, as name suggests, time spent by people on the projects and materials (license, travels, etc.) are considered as services and products. Therefore, revenue recognition process is relatively straightforward in these engagements:

- Time tracking for individuals assigned to a specific project is treated as a service obligation, and weekly time cards are sufficient for recognizing revenue in the absence of predefined milestones or deliverables.
- Essentially, the team's monthly time cards, when multiplied by their respective rates, determine the invoicing or billing amount for that month.
- Acceptance of time card details and materials/equipment (licenses, travel cost, etc.) used on a monthly basis forms the basis of revenue recognition.
- Since services are rendered continuously, the revenue is recognized proportionally to the work done and materials consumed.
- Since revenue is recognized based on the actual hours worked, any change requests (CRs) to the project scope are automatically accounted for through the time and materials logged.

Revenue recognition for Fixed Bid engagements:

A Fixed Price Commercial arrangement occurs when a client and a partner enter into a legally binding agreement in which the partner commits to delivering a product or service to the client at a specified price, within an agreed-upon timeframe, and with predefined performance obligations.

Typically, deliverables are staggered over the project timeline to allow for incremental user acceptance, with billing aligned to these delivery milestones.

Revenue recognition is based on two main factors:

- **Agreed payment milestones** with the client, and
- **Effort distribution**

Since effort distribution often changes during the project execution due to factors like missed dependencies, realized risks, scope creep, or approved Change Requests, it's crucial for the project leadership team to review these changes monthly. They should then inform the finance operations team to ensure accurate revenue recording that complies with accounting standards.

Let's take the same case study, Apex Health Insurance, and simulate multiple scenarios to understand the impact on revenue recognition during the course of Fixed Bid engagements.

Case Study - Transforming Apex Health Insurance's Customer Experience:

Apex Health Insurance, a mid-sized regional health insurance provider, is facing stiff competition from digital-first competitors. To remain competitive and improve customer satisfaction, Apex decides to undergo a digital transformation program focused on revamping their customer experience by modernizing their customer portal and mobile app. Apex invited many Service providers/partners to participate in the bidding process. After careful evolution, the work is awarded to a Partner Re-Ignite Inc **for a fixed Price of $400,000** which is expected to complete in **26 weeks.**

The agreed methodology between Apex and Re-Ignite is agile-based iterative development. There are three planned production releases, with the final deployment scheduled for week 26 of the program. The initial high-level plan and delivery/payment milestones shared during the program kick-off are as follows:

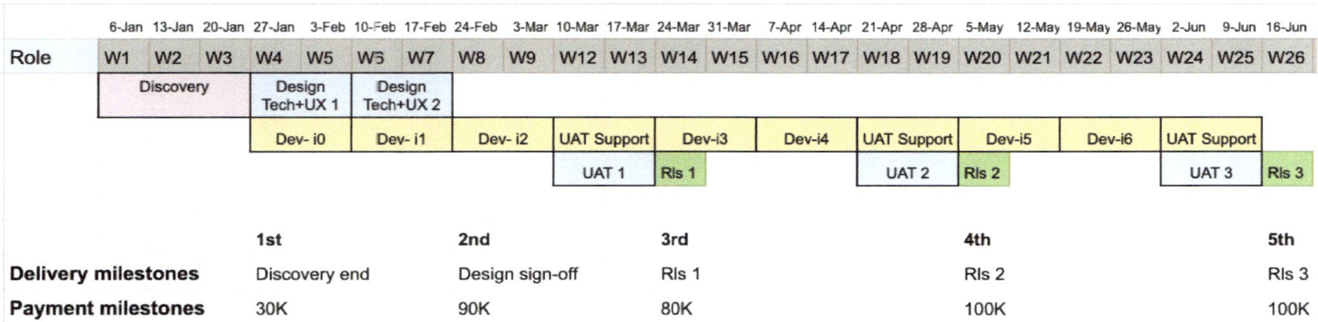

Diagram 55: Case Study - Payment & Delivery milestones

9.2 Engagement simulations for Revenue Recognition:

Let's simulate three scenarios to understand how change in team effort distribution (a.k.a., staffing plan) impacts the revenue recognition in Fixed Fee commercial arrangement.

1. Delay in Staffing during Discovery
2. Elongated UX design
3. Witnessing a legitimate Change Request

Since revenue recognition is crucial for the Partner team to ensure compliance with accounting guidelines, it's important to review some of the internal working documents related to the Re-Ignite project. These documents will help us accurately track and record revenue throughout the engagement.

When Re-Ignite prepared for the discovery workshop, they developed an initial staffing plan. This plan was based on information shared during the sales stage and their own assumptions to manage the program effectively. The initial staffing plan looks like this:

Four key roles were assumed to be staffed from Day 1 of the project to kick off the discovery workshops: Tech Lead (TL), Business Analyst (BA), Project Manager (PM), and User Experience Expert (UX). As the program progressed into design sprints and the development phase, additional roles such as Senior Developers, Developers, and Quality Engineers were planned to join according to the ramp-up schedule. Each grid showing "1" represents one week, equivalent to 5 person-days. The total staffing capacity at the beginning of the program was projected at 783 person-days.

Now, let's begin with the first scenario.

Simulation 1- Delay in staffing during Discovery

Role	W1	W2	W3	W4	W5	W6	W7	W8	W9	W12	W13	W14	W15	W16	W17	W18	W19	W20	W21	W22	W23	W24	W25	W26	Total
	6-Jan	13-Jan	20-Jan	27-Jan	3-Feb	10-Feb	17-Feb	24-Feb	3-Mar	10-Mar	17-Mar	24-Mar	31-Mar	7-Apr	14-Apr	21-Apr	28-Apr	5-May	12-May	19-May	26-May	2-Jun	9-Jun	16-Jun	
	Discovery			Design Tech+UX 1		Design Tech+UX 2																			
				Dev- i0		Dev- i1		Dev- i2		UAT Support		Dev-i3		Dev-i4		UAT Support		Dev-i5		Dev-i6		UAT Support			
										UAT 1		Rls 1				UAT 2		Rls 2				UAT 3		Rls 3	
TL	1	1	1	1	1	1	1																		35
BA	1	1	1	1	1	1	1	1	1	1	1	1													60
PM	1	1	1	1	1	1	1	1	1	1	1	1	1	1	1	1	1	1	1	1	1	1	1	1	120
UX	1	1	1	1	1	1																			30
UX				1	1	1	1																		20
Sr Dev				1	1	1	1	1	1	1	1	1	1	1	1	1	1	1	1	1	1	1	1	1	105
Sr Dev						1	1	1	1	1	1	1	1	1	1	1	1								60
Dev						1	1	1	1	1	1	1	1	1	1	1	1	1	1	1	1	1	1	1	95
Dev						1	1	1	1	1	1	1	1	1											45
Dev Risk												1	1	1	1	1	1	1							35
QE				1	1	1	1	1	1	1	1	1	1	1	1	1	1	1	1	1	1	1	1	1	105
QE																1	1	1	1						20
DevOps				0.5	0.5	0.5	0.5	0.5	0.5	0.5	0.5	0.5	0.5	0.5	0.5	0.5	0.5	0.5	0.5	0.5	0.5	0.5	0.5	0.5	52.5
Total PDs	20	20	20	38	38	53	48	38	38	38	38	43	38	38	33	38	38	33	28	23	23	23	23	23	**783**
				1st				**2nd**				**3rd**						**4th**						**5th**	
Delivery milestones				Discovery end				Design sign-off				Rls 1						Rls 2						Rls 3	
Payment milestones				30K				90K				80K						100K						100K	

Diagram 56: Case Study - Revenue Recognition Simulation- Original

Due to unavoidable circumstances, the UX expert was late in joining the project. However, the other three roles - Project Manager (PM), Tech Lead (TL), and Business Analyst (BA) - were available on the first day of discovery. After discussing the risks internally, the team decided to proceed with the discovery kick-off. The UX expert eventually joined in the last week of discovery and contributed by creating key user journeys, identifying main points, and collaborating with the team to gather insights. Despite the delay, the four-member team successfully completed the discovery phase, delivering quality outputs.

All key deliverables, including the Master Story Backlog, Project Roadmap, and key dependencies, were shared with the client, who appreciated and accepted these as the official discovery deliverables. From an effort distribution standpoint, there was a slight change during the first three weeks of discovery, with the team's total effort shifting from the planned 60 days to 50 days.

Assuming no further changes or risks are identified for the remainder of the project, the total project effort is reduced by 10 days, bringing it down from 783 to 773 person-days. This adjustment impacts the overall effort distribution and, as a result, the revenue recognition pattern also shifts, as shown in the diagram above.

Due to the reduced effort, the expected revenue recognition for the initial phase decreases from $30.6K to $25.9K. However, this adjustment results in incremental increases in subsequent revenue recognition amounts, as outlined in the table. The overall distribution ensures the project's revenue remains aligned with the revised effort, allowing for accurate financial reporting.

Simulation 2 : Elongated UX phase

	6-Jan	13-Jan	20-Jan	27-Jan	3-Feb	10-Feb	17-Feb	24-Feb	3-Mar	10-Mar	17-Mar	24-Mar	31-Mar	7-Apr	14-Apr	21-Apr	28-Apr	5-May	12-May	19-May	26-May	2-Jun	9-Jun	16-Jun	
Role	**W1**	**W2**	**W3**	**W4**	**W5**	**W6**	**W7**	**W8**	**W9**	**W12**	**W13**	**W14**	**W15**	**W16**	**W17**	**W18**	**W19**	**W20**	**W21**	**W22**	**W23**	**W24**	**W25**	**W26**	**Total**
	Discovery			Design Tech+UX 1		Design Tech+UX 2																			
				Dev- i0		Dev- i1		Dev- i2		UAT Support		Dev-i3		Dev-i4		UAT Support		Dev-i5		Dev-i6		UAT Support			
										UAT 1		Rls 1				UAT 2		Rls 2				UAT 3		Rls 3	
				1st				**2nd**				**3rd**						**4th**						**5th**	
Delivery milestones				Discovery end				Design sign-off				Rls 1						Rls 2						Rls 3	
Original staffing																									
TL	1	1	1																						
BA	1	1	1																						
PM	1	1	1																						
UX	1	1	1																						
Effort				60				175				150						225						173	**783**
Effort %				7.7%				22.3%				19.2%						28.7%						22.1%	
Planned Rev Rec				30.6 K				89.4 K				76.6 K						115 K						88.4 K	
Scenario 1 stafing																									
TL	1	1	1																						
BA	1	1	1																						
PM	1	1	1																						
UX			1																						
Effort				50				175				150						225						173	**773**
Effort %				6.5%				22.6%				19.4%						29.1%						22.4%	
Expected Rev Rec				25.9 K				90.6 K				77.6 K						116.4 K						89.5 K	

Diagram 57: Case Study - Revenue Recognition Simulation- Scenario 1

Original staffing

	6-Jan	13-Jan	20-Jan	27-Jan	3-Feb	10-Feb	17-Feb	24-Feb	3-Mar	10-Mar	17-Mar	24-Mar	31-Mar	7-Apr	14-Apr	21-Apr	28-Apr	5-May	12-May	19-May	26-May	2-Jun	9-Jun	16-Jun	
Role	**W1**	**W2**	**W3**	**W4**	**W5**	**W6**	**W7**	**W8**	**W9**	**W12**	**W13**	**W14**	**W15**	**W16**	**W17**	**W18**	**W19**	**W20**	**W21**	**W22**	**W23**	**W24**	**W25**	**W26**	**Total**
	Discovery			Design Tech+UX 1		Design Tech+UX 2																			
				Dev- i0		Dev- i1		Dev- i2		UAT Support		Dev-i3		Dev-i4		UAT Support		Dev-i5		Dev-i6		UAT Support			
										UAT 1		Rls 1				UAT 2		Rls 2				UAT 3		Rls 3	
				1st				**2nd**				**3rd**						**4th**						**5th**	
Delivery milestones				Discovery end				Design sign-off				Rls 1						Rls 2						Rls 3	
TL	1	1	1	1	1	1	1																		
BA	1	1	1	1	1	1	1	1	1	1	1	1													
PM	1	1	1	1	1	1	1	1	1	1	1	1	1	1	1	1	1	1	1	1	1	1	1	1	
UX			1	1	1	1																			
UX				1	1	1	1																		
Sr Dev				1	1	1	1	1	1	1	1	1	1	1	1	1	1	1	1	1	1	1	1	1	
Sr Dev						1	1	1	1	1	1	1	1	1	1	1	1								
Dev						1	1	1	1	1	1	1	1	1	1	1	1	1	1	1	1	1	1	1	
Dev						1	1	1	1	1	1	1	1	1											
Dev Risk												1	1	1	1	1	1	1							
QE				1	1	1	1	1	1	1	1	1	1	1	1	1	1	1	1	1	1	1	1	1	
QE																1	1	1	1						
DevOps				0.5	0.5	0.5	0.5	0.5	0.5	0.5	0.5	0.5	0.5	0.5	0.5	0.5	0.5	0.5	0.5	0.5	0.5	0.5	0.5	0.5	
Total PDs	15	15	20	38	38	53	48	38	38	38	38	43	38	38	33	38	38	33	28	23	23	23	23	23	
Effort				50				175				150						225						173	**773**
Effort %				6.5%				22.6%				19.4%						29.1%						22.4%	
Planned Rev Rec				25.9	K			90.6	K			77.6	K					116.4	K					89.5	**400K**

Scenario 2 staffing

	6-Jan	13-Jan	20-Jan	27-Jan	3-Feb	10-Feb	17-Feb	24-Feb	3-Mar	10-Mar	17-Mar	24-Mar	31-Mar	7-Apr	14-Apr	21-Apr	28-Apr	5-May	12-May	19-May	26-May	2-Jun	9-Jun	16-Jun			
Role	**W1**	**W2**	**W3**	**W4**	**W5**	**W6**	**W7**	**W8**	**W9**	**W12**	**W13**	**W14**	**W15**	**W16**	**W17**	**W18**	**W19**	**W20**	**W21**	**W22**	**W23**	**W24**	**W25**	**W26**	**W27**	**W28**	**Total**
	Discovery			Design Tech+UX 1		Design Tech+UX 2		Design Tech+UX 3																			
						Dev- i0		Dev- i1		Dev- i2		UAT Support		Dev-i3		Dev-i4		UAT Support		Dev-i5		Dev-i6		UAT Support			
												UAT 1		Rls 1				UAT 2		Rls 2				UAT 3		Rls 3	
				1st						**2nd**				**3rd**						**4th**						**5th**	
Delivery milestones				Discovery end						Design sign-off				Rls 1						Rls 2						Rls 3	
TL	1	1	1	1	1	1	1	1	1																		
BA	1	1	1	1	1	1	1	1	1	1	1	1															
PM	1	1	1	1	1	1	1	1	1	1	1	1	1	1	1	1	1	1	1	1	1	1	1	1	1	1	
UX			1	1	1	1	1	1	1																		
UX				1	1	1	1	1	1																		
Sr Dev				1	1	1	1	1	1	1	1	1	1	1	1	1	1	1	1	1	1	1	1	1	1	1	
Sr Dev						1	1	1	1	1	1	1	1	1	1	1	1	1	1								
Dev						1	1	1	1	1	1	1	1	1	1	1	1	1	1	1	1	1	1	1	1	1	
Dev						1	1	1	1	1	1	1	1	1	1												
Dev Risk												1	1	1	1	1	1	1									
QE				1	1	1	1	1	1	1	1	1	1	1	1	1	1	1	1	1	1	1	1	1	1	1	
QE																1	1	1	1	1							
DevOps				0.5	0.5	0.5	0.5	0.5	0.5	0.5	0.5	0.5	0.5	0.5	0.5	0.5	0.5	0.5	0.5	0.5	0.5	0.5	0.5	0.5	0.5	0.5	
Total PDs	15	15	20	38	38	53	53	53	53	38	38	43	38	38	38	38	38	38	33	28	23	23	23	23	5	5	**837**
Effort				**50**						**285**				**155**						**220**						**127**	
Effort %				**Done**						36.2%				19.7%						28.0%						16.1%	
Expected Rev Rec				**25.9**	K					136	K			73.7	K					104.6	K					60.2	**400K**

Diagram 58: Case Study - Revenue Recognition Simulation- Scenario 2

After a smooth discovery phase, the User Experience (UX) design phase started, but it required more iterations (3) than initially planned (2). The design phase, which was originally scheduled for 4 weeks, extended to 6 weeks, resulting in a 2-week delay in the overall project timeline. This has pushed the project duration from the planned 26 weeks to 28 weeks, and the total effort has increased from 773 to 837 person-days.

Due to the extended UX phase, the timing of the 1st, 2nd, and 3rd software releases has been shifted, impacting the payment milestones. Consequently, all revenue recognition for the remaining phases, after discovery, will need to be adjusted according to the revised effort distribution and new timeline, as outlined in the revised plan below. These adjustments ensure that the project's financial tracking remains accurate and compliant with the updated work allocation.

Due to the increased effort in the design phase, 2nd revenue recognition amount increases from $90.6K to $136K, however, this adjustment results in incremental increases in subsequent revenue recognition amounts, as outlined in the table above.

Simulation 3: Witnessing a change request

The elongated US phase invited many discussions to improve user experience for customer self servicing features. One of the self-servicing features, OTP (One-Time-Password) authentication based customer phone and address update was accepted as a new feature to be taken up as additional scope.

After discussions between the Engineering Manager and the Product Owner, it was agreed that this 'Change Request' will involve two more integrations; a change in the UI flow and some development and testing effort. The partner team provided a revised plan, including a cost estimate for the 'CR'. After a couple

Scenario 3 staffing

	6-Jan	13-Jan	20-Jan	27-Jan	3-Feb	10-Feb	17-Feb	24-Feb	3-Mar	10-Mar	17-Mar	24-Mar	31-Mar	7-Apr	14-Apr	21-Apr	28-Apr	5-May	12-May	19-May	26-May	2-Jun	9-Jun	16-Jun			
Role	**W1**	**W2**	**W3**	**W4**	**W5**	**W6**	**W7**	**W8**	**W9**	**W12**	**W13**	**W14**	**W15**	**W16**	**W17**	**W18**	**W19**	**W20**	**W21**	**W22**	**W23**	**W24**	**W25**	**W26**	**W27**	**W28**	**Total**
	Discovery			Design Tech+UX 1		Design Tech+UX 2		Design Tech+UX 3																			
						Dev- i0		Dev- i1		Dev- i2		UAT Support		Dev-i3		Dev-i4		UAT Support		Dev-i5		Dev-i6		UAT Support			
												UAT 1		Rls 1				UAT 2		Rls 2				UAT 3		Rls 3	
				1st						**2nd**				**3rd**						**4th**						**5th**	
Delivery milestones				Discovery end						Design sign-off				Rls 1						Rls 2						Rls 3	
TL	1	1	1	1	1	1	1	1	1																		
BA	1	1	1	1	1	1	1	1	1	1	1	1															
PM	1	1	1	1	1	1	1	1	1	1	1	1	1	1	1	1	1	1	1	1	1	1	1	1	1	1	
UX			1	1	1	1	1	1	1																		
UX				1	1	1	1	1	1																		
Sr Dev				1	1	1	1	1	1	1	1	1	1	1	1	1	1	1	1	1	1	1	1	1	1	1	
Sr Dev						1	1	1	1	1	1	1	1	1	1	1	1	1	1								
Dev						1	1	1	1	1	1	1	1	1	1	1	1	1	1	1	1	1	1	1	1	1	
Dev						1	1	1	1	1	1	1	1	1	1												
Dev Risk												1	1	1	1	1	1	1									
Dev CR															1	1	1	1									
QE				1	1	1	1	1	1	1	1	1	1	1	1	1	1	1	1	1	1	1	1	1	1	1	
QE																1	1	1	1	1							
DevOps				0.5	0.5	0.5	0.5	0.5	0.5	0.5	0.5	0.5	0.5	0.5	0.5	0.5	0.5	0.5	0.5	0.5	0.5	0.5	0.5	0.5	0.5	0.5	
Total PDs	15	15	20	38	38	53	53	53	53	38	38	43	38	38	43	43	43	43	33	28	23	23	23	23	5	5	**857**
Effort				**50**						**285**				**155**						**240**						**127**	
Effort %				**Done**						**Done**				**Done**						65.5%						34.5%	
Expected Rev Rec				**25.9** K						**136** K				**73.7** K						120.8 K						63.6	**420K**

Diagram 59: Case Study - Revenue Recognition Simulation- Scenario 3

of rounds of discussions, this CR is approved with a cost of $20K. An additional developer was added to address the change request, which increased the overall effort from 837 to 857 person-days. This also led to an increase in revenue by $20K. As a result, the total project revenue rose to $420K. The table below illustrates the impact of this change request on the revenue recognition pattern.

Three milestones related revenues were recognized earlier, the remaining revenue including the CR revenue was adjusted to reflect the updated effort pattern for the rest of the project as shown in the table above.

As demonstrated by the three scenarios above, the staffing plan fluctuates throughout the project based on the evolving effort needed to address risks, dependencies, and change requests. These adjustments directly impact the effort distribution, which in turn affects the revenue recognition pattern. It's essential to continuously update and adjust the revenue recognition to comply with accounting principles, ensuring accurate financial reporting and reflecting the true progress and resource utilization of the project.

Chapter 10

Glossary and Index

Glossary

Y2K: it was a computer problem in the year 2000 where people got concerned when the date changed from 31/12/99 to 01/01/00, computers using two digits for the year (like "99" for 1999) might confuse "00" for 1900, potentially causing errors in date-related tasks such as calculations, scheduling, etc.

AS/400: now called IBM, is a midrange computer system developed by IBM that combines hardware and software for business applications. It's known for its reliability, security, and ability to run multiple operating systems and applications simultaneously.

iSeries Servers: formerly known as AS/400, are a line of midrange computer systems from IBM designed for business applications. They combine processing power, storage, and database capabilities in a single system, support multiple programming languages and can run various applications, making it popular for enterprise resource planning (ERP) and other critical business functions. It's known for its reliability, security, and ease of management. iSeries servers were originally designed for small-to-medium-sized businesses that needed more processing power than a standard commodity server, but less than a mainframe.

RPG/400: stands for Report Program Generator/400. It's a version of the RPG programming language designed to run on IBM's AS/400 (later known as iSeries) systems, primarily used for business applications and data processing.

DDMMYY: is a date format where **DD** represents the two-digit day, **MM** represents the two-digit month, **YY** represents the last two digits of the year. This format was commonly used in programming languages and systems before the year 2000. This format only allocated two digits for the year (YY), which caused the Y2K problem.

DDMMYYYY: is a date format where **DD** represents the two-digit day, **MM** represents the two-digit month and **YYYY** represents the four-digit year. This format was adopted in many systems after the **Y2K problem** to avoid ambiguity in the year representation, as it uses four digits for the year instead of two, thus preventing confusion between centuries.

Ctrl+F: is a keyboard shortcut used to quickly find specific words or phrases in a document, webpage, text-based interface or any developer interface. AS/400 traditionally used a green-screen interface, where text navigation and searching were handled through specific commands or function keys rather than typical shortcuts like Ctrl+F. However, as newer development environments for the AS/400 platform evolved, the **Ctrl+F** shortcut for searching text through source code files has been introduced.

Mainframe: A mainframe is a powerful computer used mainly by large organizations for processing and managing vast amounts of data. Think of it as a super-sized, highly reliable computer that can handle thousands of tasks simultaneously. These systems are often used in industries like banking, insurance, and government, where they manage critical applications and large databases. Mainframes are known for their speed, security, and ability to support many users at once, making them essential for operations that require a lot of processing power and uptime.

Midrange Systems: they are computers that sit between mainframes and personal computers in terms of size and power. An example of a midrange machine is the IBM AS/400, which is known for its reliability and versatility in various business applications.

GUI: A GUI, or Graphical User Interface, is a visual way for users to interact with computers using elements like windows, icons, and buttons. Instead of typing commands, users can click and navigate through applications easily. GUIs are commonly found in operating systems like Windows and macOS, making software more user-friendly.

Mobile Computing: Mobile computing refers to the use of portable devices, like smartphones and tablets, to access and process information from anywhere. It works through wireless connections, letting you stay connected on the move. This makes it easy to work, browse, or chat wherever you are.

IoT: The Internet of Things (IoT) refers to everyday objects like appliances, cars, or devices that are connected to the internet. These objects can collect and share data, allowing them to communicate with each other or be controlled remotely. For example, a smart thermostat can adjust your home's temperature from your phone, or a fitness tracker can send health data to your doctor.

Cloud computing: Cloud computing is a way to store and access data or programs over the internet instead of using your computer's hard drive. It lets you use services like file storage, apps, or processing power from remote servers, so you can access them from anywhere. For example, services like Google Drive or Dropbox let you save files online and access them on any device.

SaaS: SaaS (Software as a Service) is a way to use software over the internet without needing to install it on your computer. Instead of buying and downloading software, you access it through a web browser, and the provider takes care of updates and maintenance. Examples include Amazon Prime, Netflix etc.

PaaS: PaaS (Platform as a Service) is a cloud service that provides developers with a platform to build, test, and deploy applications without worrying about the underlying infrastructure. It offers tools, operating systems, databases, and servers, so developers can focus on writing code. Examples include Google App Engine and Microsoft Azure.

IaaS: IaaS (Infrastructure as a Service) is a cloud service that provides virtual computing resources like servers, storage, and networks over the internet. Instead of buying physical hardware, businesses can rent and scale these resources as needed. Examples include Amazon Web Services (AWS), Microsoft Azure, and Google Cloud

Big data and Analytics: Big data refers to extremely large and complex sets of data that are difficult to manage with traditional methods. Analytics is the process of examining this data to discover patterns, trends, and insights. Together, big data and analytics help organizations make better decisions by analyzing vast amounts of information from various sources, such as customer behavior, social media, or business operations.

2020 Pandemic: Caused by COVID-19, it was a global health crisis that accelerated digital adoption across various sectors. With lockdowns and social distancing measures in place, businesses and consumers turned to online services, leading to a surge in e-commerce, remote work, and digital communication tools. This shift transformed how people interact, shop, and work, with lasting impacts on digital strategies and technologies.

B2C: or Business-to-Consumer, refers to the transactions and interactions between businesses and individual consumers. In this model, businesses sell products or services directly to end-users. Examples include online retailers like Amazon, streaming services like Netflix, and food delivery apps like Zomato and Swiggy.

B2B: or Business-to-Business, refers to transactions and interactions between businesses. In this model, companies sell products or services to other businesses. Examples include wholesale suppliers, software companies selling enterprise solutions, and manufacturers providing goods to retailers.

AI: or Artificial Intelligence, refers to the simulation of human intelligence in machines that are programmed to think and learn like humans. It involves technologies that enable computers to perform tasks such as understanding natural language, recognizing patterns, solving problems, and making decisions. AI is used in various applications, including virtual assistants like Siri, recommendation engine like those on Netflix, Youtube etc.

ML: or Machine Learning, is a part of artificial intelligence that allows computers to learn from data and get better over time without being told what to do. It helps machines recognize patterns and make predictions. For example, it's used in recommendations on Netflix, sorting spam emails, and recognizing faces in photos.

NLP: or Natural Language Processing, is a branch of artificial intelligence that helps computers understand, interpret, and respond to human language. It enables machines to process and analyze text or speech, making it possible for applications like chatbots, voice assistants, and translation services. For example, when you ask Siri a question or use Google Translate, that's NLP in action.

Computer Vision: Computer vision is a part of artificial intelligence that helps computers understand what they see in pictures and videos. For example, when your phone unlocks by recognizing your face, that's computer vision at work. It's also used in things like self-driving cars to see the road, apps that identify plants or animals, and even in security cameras that detect movement.

Robotics: Robotics is a field of technology that involves designing, building, and using robots to perform tasks. Robots can be programmed to do many things, like assembling products in factories, exploring other planets, or even assisting in surgeries. For example, robotic vacuum cleaners can clean your home automatically, and industrial robots can work on assembly lines to make cars

AV: or Autonomous Vehicles, are vehicles that can drive themselves without human intervention. They use a combination of sensors, cameras, and artificial intelligence to navigate and make decisions on the road. For example, self-driving cars can recognize traffic signals, avoid obstacles, and follow other vehicles. Companies like Waymo and Tesla are developing AV technology to test driver less cars to make transportation more efficient.

DORA: or DevOps Research and Assessment, is a framework that helps organizations measure and improve their software development and delivery performance. It focuses on key metrics like deployment frequency, lead time for changes, time to restore service, and change failure rate. These metrics help teams understand how effectively they're delivering software and identify areas for improvement to accelerate development and maintain high reliability.

DevOps: DevOps is a set of practices that combines software development (Dev) and IT operations (Ops) to improve collaboration and automate processes. The goal is to deliver software faster and more reliably by breaking down silos between developers and operations teams. DevOps uses tools and practices like continuous integration, continuous delivery (CI/CD), and automated testing to speed up development, reduce errors, and ensure smooth deployments.

Lean: In software, Lean focuses on reducing waste and improving efficiency in development. It emphasizes building only essential features based on user needs, speeding up delivery without sacrificing quality. By continuously improving processes, teams can release software faster and with fewer resources. Lean helps optimize coding, testing, and deployment to deliver more value to users.

TCO: or Total Cost of Ownership, refers to the complete cost of owning a product or system over its entire lifecycle. In software, this includes not just the initial purchase or development cost but also expenses like maintenance, support, upgrades, and infrastructure. TCO helps businesses understand the long-term financial impact of their technology investments. It's used to compare solutions and make informed decisions about which option offers the best value over time.

D2C: or Direct-to-Consumer, is a business model where brands sell products directly to customers without using intermediaries like retailers or wholesalers. This approach allows companies to control their branding, pricing, and customer experience while collecting valuable customer data. Examples of D2C brands include companies like **boAt**, which sells audio products like headphones and speakers directly to consumers through its website and online platforms and **Warby Parker**, known for selling eyewear directly to customers through their online store and physical locations, bypassing traditional retailers.

RFP: or Request for Proposal, is a formal document that organizations use to solicit bids from potential vendors or service providers. It outlines the project requirements, objectives, and criteria for evaluation, allowing companies to compare responses and choose the best vendor, service provider or partner. An RFP helps ensure transparency and competitiveness in the procurement process, especially for large projects or services.

CASA: or Current Account and Savings Account, refers to two types of deposit accounts offered by banks. A **Current Account** is primarily used for business transactions, allowing unlimited withdrawals and deposits, though it usually does not earn interest. It often includes features like overdraft facilities and cheque books. In contrast, a **Savings Account** is designed for individuals to save money while earning interest on their deposits, typically with restrictions on the number of withdrawals. Together, CASA accounts are crucial for banks as they provide low-cost funds for lending while attracting deposits from customers.

APIs: or Application Programming Interfaces, are protocols that allow different software applications to communicate with each other. They enable developers to access features or data from a service without needing to understand its underlying code. For instance, a weather app uses an API to get data from a weather service. APIs are crucial for modern applications, facilitating integration and enhancing functionality across systems.

UAT: or User Acceptance Testing, is the final phase of software testing where real users test the system to ensure it meets their needs and requirements. It validates that the software functions as intended in a real-world environment before it goes live. UAT helps identify any issues or necessary adjustments from the user's perspective. Successful completion of UAT signifies that the software is ready for deployment.

RCA: or Root Cause Analysis, is a technique used in software development to identify the underlying causes of bugs or issues within a system. It involves analyzing incidents to uncover the factors that led to the problem, rather than just addressing the surface symptoms. By understanding the root cause, development teams can implement effective fixes and prevent similar issues from occurring in the future. RCA is essential for improving software quality and enhancing development processes.

SEO: or Search Engine Optimization, is the practice of improving a website's visibility on search engines like Google. It involves optimizing content, keywords, and technical aspects to rank higher in search results. Effective SEO helps attract more organic traffic, making it easier for users to find relevant information.

CUG: In the context of software development, CUG, or Closed User Group, refers to a restricted group of users who have access to specific software features, applications, or environments that are not available to the general public. This is often used for beta testing or pilot programs, allowing selected users to provide feedback and identify issues before a wider release. This approach helps improve software quality and user experience before the final launch.

PROD: In software development, PROD, short for Production, refers to the live environment where the final version of software applications is deployed and accessible to end users. Any issues in the PROD environment can directly impact users and business operations, so thorough testing is conducted before deployment. Maintaining and monitoring PROD is essential to ensure a seamless user experience and uphold system reliability.

DNA: In the context of mental models, DNA represents the fundamental beliefs, experiences, and knowledge that shape how individuals perceive and interpret the world around them. Just as DNA encodes genetic information, these mental models encode our understanding, guiding decision-making and problem-solving. They influence how we approach challenges, interact with others, and adapt to new situations. Recognizing and examining our mental models can help us understand biases, improve our thinking processes, and enhance our ability to learn and grow.

Max Cap: or Maximum Cap, in Time and Materials (T&M) contracts refers to a predefined limit on the total cost that a client is willing to pay for a project. This cap provides a safeguard for clients against unexpected costs while allowing for flexibility in the project's scope and timeline.

R&D: or Research and Development, involves systematic efforts to innovate and improve software products, features, or processes. This includes exploring new technologies, conducting experiments, and developing prototypes to translate ideas into functional applications.

IPR: or Intellectual Property Rights, in software industry, protect the ownership of ideas, code, designs, and technologies created during the process. It includes copyrights, patents, and trademarks, ensuring that no one can use or copy the software without permission. IPR helps developers and companies control how their software is used and sold. This protection encourages innovation by securing their work and investments.

FTE: or Full-Time Equivalent, is a unit used to measure the workload of an employee in relation to a full-time position. One FTE equals the hours worked by one full-time employee, typically 40 hours per week. It helps organizations calculate staffing needs, compare workloads, and budget for labor costs. E.g. two part-time employees working 20 hours each would equal one FTE.

Staff augmentation: Staff augmentation is when a company hires temporary external professionals to fill skill gaps or help with extra work. These hired experts work alongside the in-house team for specific projects. It allows businesses to quickly add the right talent without hiring full-time staff. This is often used in areas like IT and software development where specialized skills are needed.

Co-sourcing: Co-sourcing is similar to staff augmentation when a company partners with an external provider to share responsibilities for certain tasks or projects. Both the in-house team and the external team work together, combining their strengths to achieve goals. It offers flexibility and access to specialized skills without fully outsourcing the work.

Scope creep: Scope creep is when a project's goals expand beyond the original plan without adjusting time or budget. It often happens when new features are added without proper approval. This can cause delays, extra costs, and strain on resources. To avoid scope creep, it's essential to set clear project boundaries and communicate well with everyone involved.

BCP: or Business Continuity Planning, is a strategy to ensure that a company can keep operating during and after a disaster or unexpected event. It involves creating plans to protect essential functions, minimize downtime, and recover quickly. BCP includes identifying potential risks and outlining steps to maintain services.

Story Points: Story points are a unit of measurement used in Agile project management to estimate the effort required to complete a user story or task. Instead of measuring time, story points consider factors like complexity, risk, and amount of work. Teams assign a point value to each story based on their understanding, often using a scale like Fibonacci numbers. This helps teams prioritize tasks, plan sprints, and gauge their progress in a more flexible and relative way.

SOW: or Statement of Work, is a formal document that outlines the specific tasks, deliverables, and timelines for a project. It clearly defines the scope of work, objectives, and responsibilities of all parties involved. An SOW helps ensure everyone is on the same page and sets expectations for what will be delivered. This document is crucial for managing projects and avoiding misunderstandings between clients and service providers.

TAT: or Turnaround Time, refers to the amount of time taken to complete a process or fulfill a request. It measures the time from when a task is started to when it is finished and delivered. Shorter TAT is often preferred, as it indicates efficiency and quicker service. Businesses use TAT to improve their operations and enhance customer satisfaction.

Tech Debt: or technical debt, refers to the shortcuts or compromises made in software development that can lead to future problems. It occurs when developers prioritize speed over quality, resulting in code that is difficult to maintain or update. While it may help meet deadlines initially, it can create bigger issues down the line, requiring more time and resources to fix. Managing tech debt is important to ensure the long-term health and efficiency of software systems.

Brownfield: Brownfield refers to improving or updating existing systems or applications instead of creating new ones from scratch. In software development, brownfield projects often involve integrating new features or technologies into legacy systems. This approach helps organizations use their current resources while enhancing functionality. Brownfield development can be more complex due to the need to work with existing code and architecture but often provides a faster path to modernization.

NPS: or Net Promoter Score, is a metric used to measure customer loyalty and satisfaction. It gauges how likely customers are to recommend a company or its products to others on a scale from 0 to 10. Customers are categorized into promoters, passives, and detractors based on their scores. NPS helps businesses understand their customers' sentiments and identify areas for improvement to enhance overall customer experience.

KPI: or Key Performance Indicator, is a measurable value used to track how well a company or project is performing. It helps assess progress toward specific goals, like sales growth or customer satisfaction. KPIs give organizations clear data to make informed decisions. By monitoring KPIs, businesses can improve their strategies and reach their objectives more effectively.

CR: or Change Request, is a formal proposal to modify a project, system, or product after its initial requirements are defined. It can involve changes to features, timelines, or resources. CRs ensure that changes are reviewed, approved, and documented properly. Managing CRs helps keep projects on track while accommodating necessary adjustments.

TTM: or Time to Market, is the amount of time it takes to develop a product from the idea stage to when it's available for customers. Faster TTM helps companies stay competitive and respond quickly to market demands. It's an important measure for efficiency in product development. Reducing TTM can lead to quicker profits and a stronger market presence.

CBA: or Cost-Benefit Analysis, is a process used to compare the costs and benefits of a project or decision. It helps determine whether the benefits outweigh the costs and if the project is worth pursuing. This analysis helps businesses make informed decisions by evaluating potential gains and risks.

MVP: or Minimum Viable Product, is the simplest version of a product that has just enough features to satisfy early users. It's released quickly to gather feedback and test the idea before fully developing it. This helps companies reduce risks and make improvements based on real user input.

CMS: or Content Management System, is a software platform that allows users to create, manage, and modify digital content on websites without needing technical expertise. It simplifies tasks like editing text, adding images, or updating pages. Popular CMS platforms include WordPress and Joomla. Using a CMS helps businesses maintain their websites easily and efficiently.

ESB: or Enterprise Service Bus, is a software architecture that helps different applications communicate with each other. It acts as a central hub, allowing systems to exchange data without needing direct connections. ESB simplifies integration, making it easier for businesses to manage and connect various software applications. This is especially useful in large organizations with multiple systems that need to work together efficiently.

MoSCoW: is a prioritization technique used in project management to categorize tasks into four groups: Must have, Should have, Could have, and Won't have. It helps teams focus on the most important requirements first. "Must have" items are essential, while "Should" and "Could" are less critical but desirable. "Won't have" items are not needed for now. This method ensures that key goals are met within deadlines and resources.

ROI: or Return on Investment, measures the profitability of an investment by comparing the gains to the costs. A higher ROI means the investment is more profitable. Businesses use ROI to evaluate the success of projects or investments and make informed financial decisions.

ARR: or Annual Recurring Revenue, is the amount of predictable revenue a business expects to generate each year from subscriptions or long-term contracts. It's commonly used by subscription-based companies to measure their financial health. ARR helps track growth and predict future revenue.

CSAT: or Customer Satisfaction Score, is a measure used to gauge how satisfied customers are with a product or service. It's typically collected through surveys asking customers to rate their experience on a scale. A higher CSAT indicates better customer satisfaction and loyalty. Businesses use CSAT to identify areas for improvement and enhance the overall customer experience.

CTAs: or Call to Actions, are prompts that encourage users to take a specific action, such as signing up for a newsletter or making a purchase. They are often used in marketing and on websites to guide users toward desired outcomes. Effective CTAs are clear, compelling, and visually distinct to grab attention. By using CTAs, businesses can improve engagement and conversion rates.

WBS: or Work Breakdown Structure, is a project management tool that breaks a project into smaller, manageable tasks. It helps organize and define the scope of work required to complete a project. Each level of the WBS provides more detail, making it easier to plan and allocate resources. Using a WBS helps ensure that all aspects of a project are covered and improves overall project tracking.

SOAP: or Simple Object Access Protocol, is a messaging protocol used for exchanging structured information between systems over the internet. It relies on XML to format the messages, making it platform-independent and compatible with various programming languages. SOAP is commonly used in web services to enable communication between applications. This protocol ensures reliable communication and can support security and transaction features.

CRM: or Customer Relationship Management, is a system that helps businesses manage their interactions with customers. It stores customer information, tracks sales, and organizes communication to improve relationships and service. CRM tools enable companies to analyze customer data and tailor their marketing strategies. By using CRM, businesses can enhance customer satisfaction and drive sales growth.

PERT: or Program Evaluation and Review Technique, is a project management tool used to plan and analyze tasks within a project. It helps estimate the time needed to complete each task by considering optimistic, pessimistic, and most likely durations. PERT diagrams visually represent the project's timeline and dependencies, making it easier to identify critical paths. This technique helps ensure projects are completed on time by managing uncertainties in scheduling.

RPN: or Risk Priority Number, is a metric used in risk management to assess and prioritize potential risks in a project. It is calculated by multiplying three factors: the likelihood of the risk occurring, the impact of the risk if it occurs, and the ability to detect the risk before it happens. A higher RPN indicates a greater priority for addressing that risk. By using RPN, teams can focus their efforts on the most critical risks to improve project success.

WIFME: or "What's In It For Me," is a concept used to identify the benefits or value a person can gain from a particular action or decision. It helps motivate individuals by highlighting how something will positively impact their lives or goals. Understanding WIFME is essential in marketing, communication, and change management. By addressing this question, businesses can better engage their audience and drive desired actions.

AEM: or Adobe Experience Manager, is a content management solution that helps businesses create, manage, and optimize customer experiences across different channels. It allows users to build websites, mobile apps, and forms easily without extensive coding knowledge. By using AEM, companies can deliver consistent and relevant content to their audience efficiently.

GAAP: or Generally Accepted Accounting Principles, is a set of accounting standards and guidelines used in the U.S. to ensure consistency and transparency in financial reporting. These principles cover various aspects of accounting, including how to record revenue, expenses, and assets. Adhering to GAAP is essential for maintaining trust with investors, regulators, and stakeholders.

10.2 Diagram Index

Diagram 1: Mental Model of the Book

Diagram 2: The fast-evolving world of Digital Transformation

Diagram 3: Development Methodolgies

Diagram 4: Survey Response - Question 1

Diagram 5: Survey Response - Question 2

Diagram 6: Survey Response - Question 3

Diagram 7: Survey Response - Question 5

Diagram 8: Survey Response - Question 6

Diagram 9: Survey Response - Question 9

Diagram 10: Client's Maturity Spcctrum - A Graphical View

Diagram 11: Client's Maturity Spectrum - A Tabular View

Diagram 12: Partner's Maturity Spectrum - A Graphical View

Diagram 13: Partner's Maturity Spectrum - A Tabular View

Diagram 14: Key Stakeholders of Digital Transformation

Diagram 15: Done is better than Perfect Vs First Time Right

Diagram 16: Common Commercial Models

Diagram 17: Common Commercial Models - A Comparison View

Diagram 18: The Variants of Fixed Bid Models

Diagram 19: The Variants of Fixed Bid Models - A Comparison View

Diagram 20: The Principles of Outcome-based Commercial Models

Diagram 21: The Key Digital Transformation Metrics

Diagram 22: The Key Digital Transformation Metrics - An Illustrative example

Diagram 23: Variable Payout Calculation - An Illustrative example

Diagram 24: Common Myths of Fixed Bid Program

Diagram 25: Win-Win-Win Model of a Large Transformation Program

Diagram 26: Shared Understanding of Program Goals and Scope

Diagram 27: Case Study - Program Metrics

Diagram 28: Case Study - High Level Scope

Diagram 29: Low Fidelity Concepts - An illustrative example

Diagram 30: Case Study - Solution WBS

Diagram 31: Case Study - Program Assumptions

Diagram 32: Alignment on Ways of Working

Diagram 33: Case Study - Dependency Matrix

Diagram 34: Case Study - Sign-off Matrix

Diagram 35: An Example of Light Weight Change Request Management Process

Diagram 36: A Pragmatic Approach towards Estimation and Planning

Diagram 37: Case Study - Bottom up Estimations

Diagram 38: Case Study - Town down Estimations

Diagram 39: Case Study - Reconciliation between Top-down and Bottom-up estimates

Diagram 40: Understand Trade-offs

Diagram 41: Case Study - Program Trade-offs

Diagram 42: Continuous Value Articulation

Diagram 43: Case Study - Program Metrics Articulation - An Illustrative example

Diagram 44: Case Study - Program Dashboard Framework - An Illustrative example

Diagram 45: Well Begun is Half Done

Diagram 46: Understand People behind their Roles

Diagram 47: Baselining Efforts

Diagram 48: Collaborative Workshops than Meetings

Diagram 49: Heatmap based Risk Register

Diagram 50: RPN based Risk Register

Diagram 51: People Growth Tracker - An illustrative example

Diagram 52: Case Study - Light Weight Decision Log - An Illustrative example

Diagram 53: Louise Framework of Resistance

Diagram 54: Revenue Recognition Method in Software Services

Diagram 55: Case Study - Payment and Delivery Milestones

Diagram 56: Case Study - Revenue Recognition Simulation - Original

Diagram 57: Case Study - Revenue Recognition Simulation - Scenario 1

Diagram 58: Case Study - Revenue Recognition Simulation - Scenario 2

Diagram 59: Case Study - Revenue Recognition Simulation - Scenario 3

References

Bringselius, L. D. (2010) 'Resistance to change: Four interpretations', Lund University, Department of Business Administration. Address: Box 7080, SE-220 07 Lund, SWEDEN E-mail: louise.bringselius@fek.lu.se

Dannemiller, K.D. & Jacobs, R.W. (1992). 'Changing the way organizations change: A revolution of common sense', *Journal of Applied Behavioral Science*, **28**(4), pp. 480–498